NOURISHMENTS

Heart of Mercy

•BIBLE STUDY BY•

DEBORAH BUCKINGHAM

 Published by Gregory and Deborah Buckingham. They can be reached at soulnourishments@gmail.com

First Printing, 2017
ISBN 978-1-7326688-4-3

Printed in the United States of America
14 13 12 11 10 / 10 9 8 7 6 5 4 3 2 1

Contents

preface

the plan

Welcome to The Heart of Mercy!

I had no idea how incredibly significant mercy was to Jesus and how much He wants us to live merciful lives until I went through a season of conflict with others who challenged me to not just know about mercy, but to practice it. I learned a lot (through both my studying and my trying to live out) and I am so excited to share it with you.

This study means so much to me. The past nine years have been a season of growth where the Lord has given me opportunities to learn and practice the better, more merciful way of being with others. I seem to have encountered one difficult incident after another with people I thought I could trust and respect. In the conflict I found myself at a crossroads; Do I forgive them and show mercy or do I become bitter and angry? I began to wonder: How does one navigate these choppy waters with integrity while at the same time choose to honor the Lord with a merciful spirit?

Do you ever find yourself at this same crossroads?

We Christians have a great opportunity to live out our faith when we are hurting emotionally or physically. I believe this is why Jesus told the leaders of His day in Matthew 9 that He didn't come to earth to witness their religious practices, but rather He came to teach mercy, and they should learn what it means. Wow! That is powerful, isn't it?

God has wonderful plans for you and me, but we can get stuck and never realize His great plans if we don't understand what He requires of us. As you will discover, mercy is very important to God. As we work through this guide, we will learn exactly what it means to show mercy and how our daily choices either grow or inhibit this important spiritual discipline.

This study guide is accompanied by a six-session video teaching series. Ideally, participants will complete the study individually, then join with their small group to watch the video and discuss the study guide questions together.

May our good and gracious Lord speak to our heart of hearts and teach us to live with mercy, just as He did.

—Be Nourished and Be Merciful,

Deborah Buckingham

WEEK

One

WHAT IS MERCY?

A story of mercy . . . "Now Naaman, commander of the army of the king of Syria, was a great and honorable man in the eyes of his master, because by him the Lord had given victory to Syria. He was also a mighty man of valor, but a leper. And the Syrians had gone out on raids, and had brought back captive a young girl from the land of Israel. She waited on Naaman's wife. Then she said to her mistress, "If only my master were with the prophet who is in Samaria! For he would heal him of his leprosy." And Naaman went in and told his master, saying, "Thus and thus said the girl who is from the land of Israel." Then the king of Syria said, "Go now, and I will send a letter to the king of Israel."

2 Kings 5: 1-5, NKJV

Here we see an innocent young girl from Israel, kidnapped from her home, snatched from familiar customs and language, and taken to a foreign land with a foreign god. Can you imagine how terrified she must have been? Her life as a female slave would not have been valued at this time in history and in this culture, and yet we see God using her to display His mercy to the undeserving.

She had the ear of a powerful man's wife. No doubt, God had prepared her in advance, in her parents' home, with an understanding of how personal and powerful the One True God is. When we call upon Him, God is always working for good, even if the circumstances seem really bad. She understood this about her God. We see in this story her strong faith and her hope in Him. She viewed her problems as opportunities to share her Lord and show mercy.

The most amazing thing about this story is that she cared enough to want to help her captor. We would understand if she were angry and bitter instead of loving and caring. Yet, she loved her enemy and reached out to help him; this is mercy! She most certainly had the love of God in her heart. Equally amazing is that Naaman considered her advice! Why would he pay any mind to this young captive female? Could it be she caught his attention by the attitude she displayed in her circumstances? She was the fragrant aroma of God Almighty! God is a merciful God and reaches out to His enemies with love and mercy, and this young girl amazingly did the same!

Mercy—What is it? Why is it important, and how can you and I recognize God's mercy in our lives? How important is it that we show mercy? Are you merciful?

Many theologians arguably believe mercy is God's number one characteristic. In fact some call the Attributes of God the Mercies of God.

Mercy is like the umbrella that covers the characteristics of God.

Often we hear mercy and grace together. Are the two identical?

Grace is God giving me what I don't deserve.

Mercy is God not giving me what I do deserve.

It is only by the grace of God and His favor and kindness upon us that we are invited to have a relationship with Him. His good will and loving-kindness are all God's gifts of grace. For it is by grace you have been saved, through faith—and this is not from yourselves, it is the gift of

God—not by works, so that no one can boast. (Ephesians 2:8-9 NIV)

"There is no condemnation [God now approves and accepts you] for those who are in Christ Jesus." (Romans 8:1 NIV)

By God's grace, I am fully accepted into His family, when I receive Jesus Christ as my Lord and Savior. Because of His grace, I do not stand before Him condemned, but accepted! However, even though I now have God's Holy Spirit in me to help me and conform me into His image, this side of heaven I will still struggle with sin. I have a new Spirit within me, His Holy Spirit, but I still have a damaged heart that needs to be healed and a mind that needs to be transformed.

The great news is we don't need to walk our walk as a Christian in our own strength. We have this amazing power source we can tap into at any time.

Do you think that the Scripture says to no purpose that the [human] spirit which He has made to dwell in us lusts with envy? But He gives us more and more grace [through the power of the Holy Spirit to defy sin and live an obedient life that reflects both our faith and our gratitude for our salvation].(James 4:5-6 AMP)

We can demonstrate Mercy, for instance, by (1) showing kindness and compassion toward someone by recognizing a need and fulfilling their need and (2) through choosing to forgive another.

Mercy is what we express when we are led by the Holy Spirit to be compassionate in our attitudes, words, and actions.

Mercy is more than feeling sympathy for someone. Powered by love, mercy acts in order to spare someone from harm, pain, and suffering.

Our Lord assures us in Lamentations 3:23 (NIV) that "His mercies are new every day; great is His faithfulness toward us." Every day our Lord meets our needs, and every day He forgives our sins; this is mercy!

His mercy helps us continue in an intimate relationship with Him because sin breaks our intimacy with God. I once heard a story of a lady who said, "Lord, thank You for this perfect day and that I have no sin to confess. Well, now I think I better get out of bed and start this day."

Grace means we don't need to pay off our past with our future.

We know that sin breaks intimacy. If my husband and I are planning to snuggle on the couch and watch a movie and he does something rude, all of a sudden I don't want to snuggle with him! But, if he says he is sorry, I want to get back to the movie with him at my side. Remember the mercy seat in the Tabernacle? The mercy seat was a slab of gold, a lid, on top of the Ark of the Covenant found in the Holy of Holies on which rested the cloud or divine Presence of God. This is where God demonstrated mercy to the people of Israel. When the High Priest sprinkled the blood on the mercy seat, God would show mercy and forgive and cover (God covered for their sins) and remove their sins as far as the east is from the west. The Greek word for "mercy seat" is a metaphor for the removal of sin.

▸Look up 1 John 1:9 and 1 John 4:10.
What must we do to be forgiven?

▸Look up Romans 3:23.
What do you think it means to fall short of God's glory?

We are washed clean by the blood of Jesus, we are always forgiven. Mercy forgives. However, we are still left with the natural consequences of our sins. His mercy helps us live through the consequences, and because of His mercy, He even promises to work out the consequences for our good by not giving us what we deserve. We don't deserve to see such good from bad choices, but that is exactly what our merciful Lord promises us. Mercy takes away much of the pain for our deserved punishment.

In the Old Testament, *mercy* is most often translated as "loving-kindness" or "to show kindness". In the New Testament, *mercy* is most often translated as "compassion". In both the Old and New Testaments, *mercy* implies a personal involvement in a relationship beyond what is expected, even beyond what is fair. Mercy is love in action.

▸Will you make it a daily practice to ask the Lord to open your eyes to His mercies toward you?

Consider the words of the apostle Paul:

I thank Christ Jesus our Lord, who has given me strength to do his work. He considered me trustworthy and appointed me to serve him, even though I used to blaspheme the name of Christ. In my insolence, I persecuted his people. But God had mercy on me because I did it in ignorance and unbelief. Oh, how generous and gracious our Lord was! He filled me with the faith and love that come from Christ Jesus. This is a trustworthy saying, and everyone should accept it: "Christ Jesus came into the world to save sinners"—and I am the worst of them all. But God had mercy on me so that Christ Jesus could use me as a prime example of his great patience with even the worst sinners. Then others will realize that they, too, can believe in him and receive eternal life.
(1 Timothy 1:12-16, NLT)

▸How encouraging do you find Paul's words of thanksgiving for God's mercy?

Later when Jesus was eating supper at Matthew's house with his close followers, a lot of disreputable characters (tax collectors and sexually immoral) came and joined them. When the Pharisees saw him keeping this kind of company, they had a fit, and lit into Jesus' followers. "What kind of example is this from your Teacher, acting cozy with crooks and riffraff?" Jesus, overhearing, shot back, "Who needs a doctor: the healthy or the sick? Go figure out what this Scripture means: 'I'm after mercy, not religion.' I'm here to invite outsiders, not coddle insiders. (Matthew 9:10-13 MSG)

Jesus told us to figure out what mercy means. Jesus was referencing an Old Testament passage from Hosea which reads:

> For I desired mercy, and not sacrifice; and the knowledge of God more than burnt offerings. (Hosea 6:6, KJV)

Loving God and loving others was always God's purpose for His people. We can't love God until we spend time getting to know Him. We, like the Pharisees, won't show mercy for others until we know God. Jesus said He was after mercy and shows us where to find mercy; we start by knowing God.

▸What is the difference between knowing *about* God and *knowing* God?

Sadly, over time, the Israelites fell out of love with God and began to worship false gods. They continued to offer sacrifices and attend temple ceremonies on special holidays, but their hearts were far from Him. Like the Pharisees, they still knew about Him, but they no longer knew Him.

▸Describe a time when you found yourself busy doing "God's work" but feeling like you were not in "God's presence?"

And so the Lord says, "These people say they are mine. They honor me with their lips, but their hearts are far from me. And their worship of me is nothing but man-made rules learned by rote." (Isaiah 29:13, NLT)

Pastor Greg Laurie of Harvest Church in California and lead speaker for the Harvest Crusades, one of the largest Christian outreaches in the world, says, "I think there are a lot of people running around today who think they are Christians but really are not. They may believe in the right things, but they don't act on those beliefs. [...] There are a lot of people who are trying to live in two worlds. They know what is true. They effectively believe it is true. But they have not turned from darkness to light."

Greg Laurie, Online Daily Devotional, May 2016, Darkness to Light. 2017 Harvest Christian Fellowship.

When we turn from darkness to light, we are turning from our limited, misguided, and humanistic ways --the ways of our culture-- to the ways of Jesus. How will we ever know the path to choose if we don't know The Way that Jesus taught?

A friendship begins by learning someone's name and recognizing that person.

▸Do you know the names of God?
Check out the names of God at the end of this chapter.

▸When you hear things from social media, the news, or other sources, how do you discern truth from lies? Do you know God and His Word well enough to know what He would say about a particular issue?

After learning a person's name, the next level in a relationship is to become acquainted with the person by spending time with him or her. You begin to gather more information and learn what is important to that person. If there is a common bond after recognizing someone and becoming acquainted, the relationship moves into the friendship stage. Friends spend time together, talk to one another, have mutual interests, trust one another, have each other's backs, and have a mutual affection toward one another.

▸How would you describe the level of intimacy in your relationship with Jesus?

▸Read John 15:12-17. Imagine Jesus is saying these words directly to you. What thoughts come to mind?

▸ **Read Hebrews 13:16. What kind of sacrifices does God require of us?**

Jesus said, "I'm here to invite outsiders, not coddle insiders." Whom do you think He is referring to when He says "outsiders?" Could they be our Muslim neighbor, the gay couple around the corner, the coworker who curses nonstop? Would you consider inviting them to have a cup of coffee with you?

▸ **Can you share a time when you reached out to an "outsider" or an unbeliever?**

▸ **Who are the Christian insiders in our day? What does coddling these insiders look like?**

If you're involved in a church, do you find you have less contact with nonbelievers? In light of Jesus' words "I am here to invite outsiders, not coddle insiders" Consider what you can do to spend some time with nonbelievers. What will you do to make that happen?

▸ **Will you ask the Lord to help you reach out to someone who needs to know Jesus? Who comes to mind?**

My husband and I were recently on a road trip, and I told him, "I am so over a group of unbelievers we know." I told him I was tired of the cursing, the misguided priorities, and worldly focus. I then hit play on a podcast I saved for our trip, and the pastor talked about how Jesus came to seek and to save the lost, and we demonstrate mercy by doing the same.

I was deeply convicted and turned to my husband and said, "Ok, I am so not over them."

Jesus told us, "The Son of Man came to seek and save those who are lost" (Luke 19:10, NLT).

▸Why did Jesus say He came to earth?

Jesus told His followers what He wants us to do before He departed the earth and ascended to heaven. He said, "But you will receive power when the Holy Spirit comes on you; and you will be my witnesses in Jerusalem, and in all Judea and Samaria, and to the end of the earth" (Acts 1:8 NIV).

▸Who is the *you* in this verse? Is it your friend? Is it your pastor? Is it someone with the gift of evangelism? Replace the word you with your name and read the verse aloud. What comes to mind as you do this?

Evangelism is not for a select few or for someone with the gift of evangelism. It is my calling, and it is your calling. Jesus came and sat with others, listened to others, and cared for others.

Evangelism isn't a program. It is an overflow of a life that connects with Jesus. I connect with Him, and out of that overflow I reach out to others. We talk about what we care about; we share with others about what we love and what is in our hearts. Jesus said, "Out of the overflow of the heart speaks the mouth" (Luke 6:45, NIV). Doesn't it make sense that if you love Jesus, at some point you will talk about Him with others?

That is what people who first encountered Jesus did:

"Andrew, Simon Peter's brother, was one of the two who heard what John had said and who had followed Jesus. The first thing Andrew did was to find his brother Simon and tell him, "We have found the Messiah" (John 1:40-41, NIV). The first thing Andrew did after coming into contact with the Truth—with Jesus—was to run and tell his brother.

Will you say, "I am God's masterpiece"? Wow, chew on that one for a few days! God Himself knit you together in your mother's womb and you are His incredible work of art! Will you say, "Thank You, Jesus!"?

For, there is one God and one Mediator who can reconcile God and humanity—the man Christ Jesus. (1 Timothy 2:5, NLT)

How will people be saved? They will be saved through YOU. Every encounter with an unbeliever is an opportunity to be the fragrant aroma of Christ. Christ manifests as a living presence in your heart and shows up as kindness, gentleness, perseverance in suffering, hope, love, and joy. The world knows little of these character traits of Christ. You and I are called to imitate Jesus and reach out, stop and listen to unbelievers, and care about them. We are not to imitate the self-righteous, better-than-thou Pharisees. God saved you and me so that we will become more like Jesus and care about the same things He cares about. "For God knew his people in advance, and He chose them to become like His Son." (Romans 8:29, NLT)

His Son came to seek and save the lost. "When Jesus went ashore, He saw a large crowd [waiting], and He was moved with compassion (mercy) for them because they were like sheep without a shepherd [lacking guidance]; and He began to teach them many things." (Mark 6:34, AMP)

▸What is one way you can show compassion and mercy to those who are like sheep without a shepherd?

▸Spend some time in prayer. Ask Him to empower you with His Holy Spirit to be a witness to those in your life.

Remember, God does not call the equipped, He equips the called, and that is YOU.

"For we are God's masterpiece. He has created us anew in Christ Jesus, so we can do the good things he planned for us long ago." (Ephesians 2:10, NLT) Please put your name in this verse where there is a "we" or an "us."

day four

The best way to become a merciful person is to focus on what is important to God. A merciful person is moved to reach out to others. Being a merciful person is a manifestation of spiritual maturity- not how many Bible verses I can quote or my title within my church–it is about how much I value others. Being a merciful person is about so much more than being "good." Being merciful is seeing others through the eyes of Jesus, and then doing what He would do for them, including helping them and forgiving them. I used to tell my kids, "Every person matters because every person matters to God." What changes do we need to make to see our family, our neighbors, our friends, our politicians, and even our enemies through the lens of Jesus? Do we need to confess our sins of pride, anger, bitterness, busyness, or indifference?

The Lord wants us to know Him intimately, and He desires us to have a heart for the lost and the needy. He clearly tells us what He requires of us this side of glory. "O people, the Lord has told you what is good, and this is what He requires of you: to do what is right, to love mercy, and to walk humbly with your God." (Micah 6:8 NLT).

"What sorrow awaits you teachers of religious law and you Pharisees. Hypocrites! For you are careful to tithe even the tiniest income from your herb gardens, but you ignore the more important aspects of the law—justice, mercy, and faith. You should tithe, yes, but do not neglect the more important things. Blind guides! You strain your water so you won't accidentally swallow a gnat, but you swallow a camel" (Matthew 23:23-24, NLT).

Jesus challenged the religious leaders by telling them they focused on the unimportant things in life (gnats), but ignored the significant matters of life (camels), matters like mercy, for instance. Are you focused on the gnat while forsaking the camel? How easy it is to waste our days on Facebook, indulging ourselves with travel, food and entertainment or focusing on upward mobility. We focus on looking important within our church and forget weightier matters like mercy.

‣ **What does it mean to have a saved soul but a wasted life?**

‣ **What small and inconsequential things (gnats) tend to distract you from more important aspects of faith?**

For so many years, I viewed Abba Father as a wrathful Father who was ready to zap me the second I stepped out of line. He is, after all a God of justice and righteousness. I didn't understand that He is also a God of incredible mercy, grace and love. He gives you and me 10,000 mercies for every one judgment. And even when He does discipline us, He does so with such mercy!

Perhaps like me, you had or have an incomplete understanding of our Abba Father. I encourage you to chew on His words.

"The Lord is compassionate and merciful, slow to get angry and filled with unfailing love" (Psalm 103:8 NLT).

"For as the heavens are high above the earth, So great is His mercy toward those who fear Him" (Psalm 103:11 NKJV).

"How kind the Lord is! How good he is! So merciful, this God of ours!"(Psalm 116:5, NLT).

Remember, our goal is not to just save our souls but to also show people mercy. How does our kindness and compassion for others plant seeds in OUR own souls?

‣ **How do you define mercy?**

Perhaps like me, you had or have an incomplete understanding of our Abba Father. I encourage you to chew on His words He wrote to us.

Names

Father:

The Old Testament covers about 1500 years, and God is called "Father" only seven times. Then Jesus came along and said, "This is how you should pray, call God 'Father'.". Jesus used Father more than 150 Times to refer to God!

Jehovah:
I AM, The ONE

- Exodus 3:13-15
- Psalm 102:27, 105:1-7
- Jeremiah 16:19-21
- John 8:58

Jehovah Raah:
The Lord My Shepherd
(Raah is also translated "companion" or "friend.")

- Psalm 23
- John 10:11, 27-28
- Revelation 7:17
- Isaiah 40:11
- Matthew 18:12-13

Jehovah Shalom:
Lord My Peace

- Psalm 23
- Isaiah 26:3-4
- Isaiah 9:6
- Judges 6:24
- Ephesians 2:14-18
- Colossians 1:19-20

Jehovah Rapha:
Lord My Healer

- Exodus 15:26
- Psalm 23
- Psalm 103:1-4
- Psalm 147:3
- Isaiah 53:4-5
- Matthew 8:16-17

Adonai:
Lord and Master

- Genesis 18:27
- Exodus 34:9
- Judges 6:15
- Nehemiah 1:11
- Psalm 2:4
- Psalm 39:7
- Isaiah 21:6
- Daniel 9:9

Jehova Nissi:
The Lord My Banner of Love and Protection

- Exodus 17:15-16
- Psalm 60:4
- Isaiah 11:10
- Psalm 20:5-8
- Corinthians 15:56-57

# of God

Jehovah Tsidkenu:
The Lord My Righteousness

- Jeremiah 23:5-6 and 33:16
- Romans 3:21-22
- 2 Corinthians 5:21
- 1 John 1:7, 9

El Roi:
The God Who Sees

- Genesis 16:7-13
- Psalm 33:13-15
- Proverbs 15:3

Jehovah Sabaoth:
Lord My Protector

- Psalm 46:7
- Psalm 95:7
- Psalm 121:4
- Psalm 31:7, 15, 23
- Psalm 91:14-15
- John 17:10-12
- Acts 26:22
- Revelation 3:10

Elohim:
The Most High God

- Genesis 14:18-22
- Numbers 24:6
- Deuteronomy 32:8
- Psalm 57:2 and 78:35
- Daniel 5: 18, 21

El Shaddai:
God Almighty

- Genesis 17:1; 28:3, 35:11, 43:14, 48:3
- Exodus 6:3, Numbers 24:4
- Ruth 1:20-21
- Psalm 68:14
- Isaiah 13:6
- Joel 1:15

Jehovah Jireh:
The Lord My Provider

- Genesis 22:8, 13-14
- Romans 8:32
- Philippians 4:19
- Acts 14:7
- 1 Timothy 6:17

Jehovah Shammah:
The Lord is There

- Matthew 18:20
- Deuteronomy 31:6
- Joel 1:15

What is Mercy?:

1. Mercy is showing ____________ and ____________ toward someone by recognizing a need and ____________ their need.

2. Mercy is also choosing to ____________ another.

3. Mercy develops a ____________ with others and with God.

4. Mercy grows in our heart when we know God.

5. Intimacy with God impacts our ____________.

See how very much our Father loves us, for He calls us His children, and that is what we are! (1 John 3:1)

6. You may see yourself as ordinary but the Truth is, God considers you His ____________.

▸ **What untrue statement about yourself have you believed that you need to replace with truth from God?**

WEEK

two

THE MERCIFUL DO NOT HAVE A JUDGMENTAL SPIRIT

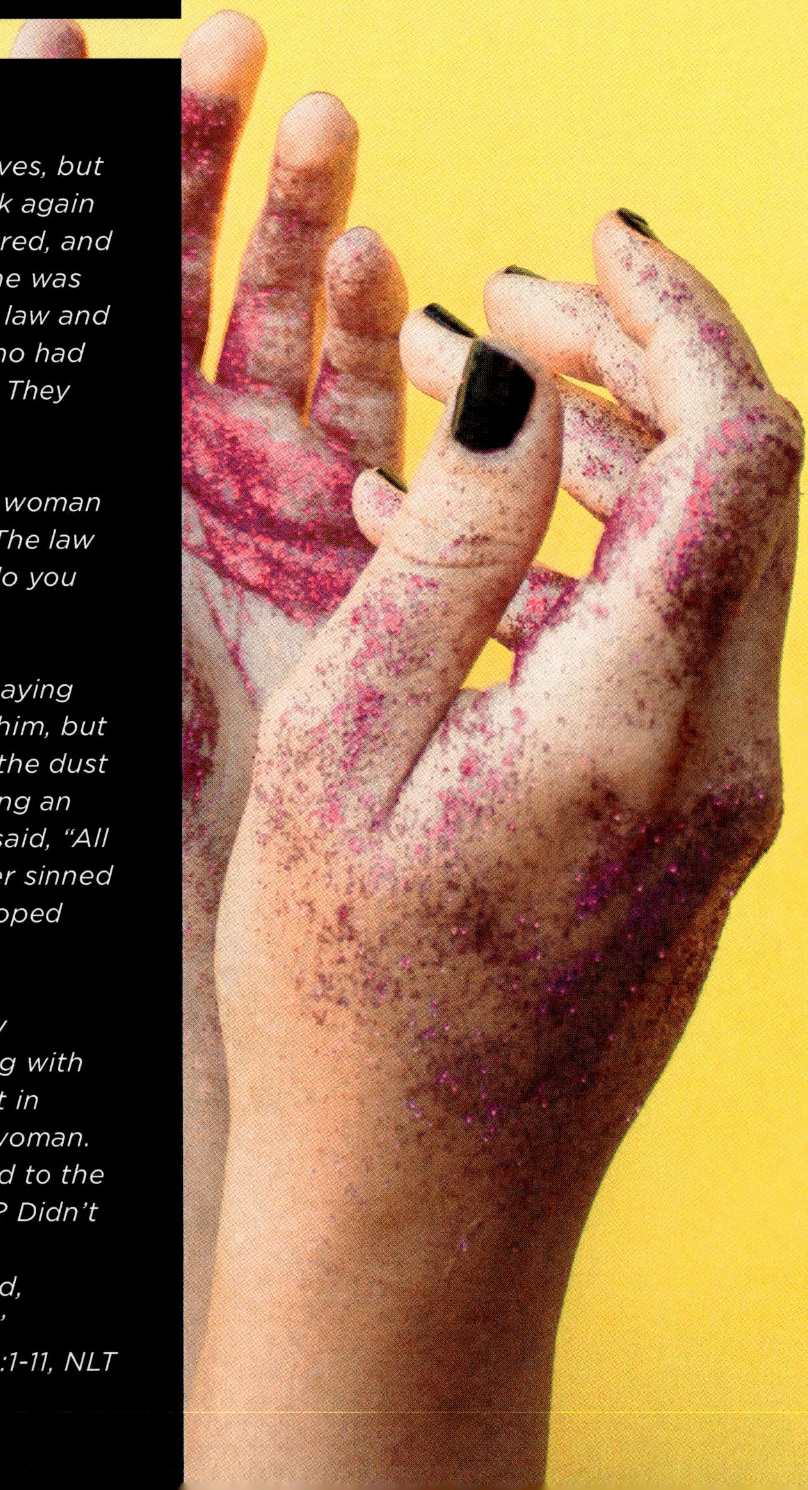

A Woman Caught in Adultery
Jesus returned to the Mount of Olives, but early the next morning he was back again at the temple. A crowd soon gathered, and he sat down and taught them. As he was speaking, the teachers of religious law and the Pharisees brought a woman who had been caught in the act of adultery. They put her in front of the crowd.

"Teacher," they said to Jesus, "this woman was caught in the act of adultery. The law of Moses says to stone her. What do you say?"

They were trying to trap him into saying something they could use against him, but Jesus stooped down and wrote in the dust with his finger. They kept demanding an answer, so he stood up again and said, "All right, but let the one who has never sinned throw the first stone!" Then he stooped down again and wrote in the dust.

When the accusers heard this, they slipped away one by one, beginning with the oldest, until only Jesus was left in the middle of the crowd with the woman. Then Jesus stood up again and said to the woman, "Where are your accusers? Didn't even one of them condemn you?"
"No, Lord," she said. And Jesus said, "Neither do I. Go and sin no more."

John 8:1-11, NLT

Here we have Jesus teaching in the temple, and the teachers and leaders storm in, dragging a terrified woman behind them. Using (rather, misusing) the Law of Moses, they ask for Jesus to approve of stoning her to death. Not exactly a picture of mercy, is it?

Remember our first point, mercy cares about what is important to God, and people are the most important thing to God. These leaders didn't care about this woman at all and had absolutely zero mercy for her. They cared about themselves and wanted to make Jesus look bad in front of His followers. They wanted to discredit Jesus. They wanted to damage His reputation. They used the Law of Moses, thinking if Jesus set the woman free, He didn't know or uphold the Torah; if He called her to be stoned, He would be usurping Roman law (John 18:31).

It is important to understand the difference between the Old Testament and New Testament. The Old Testament is called the "Old" because, as believers, we have a New Covenant with God. Under the Old Covenant Law, Israel was a theocracy. There are no theocracies today, and Christians today do not live under the civil laws outlined in the Old Testament. Christians today also do not live under the ceremonial laws in the Old Testament meant to prepare believers for worship in the Temple. We do, however, live under the moral laws mentioned in the Old Testament and repeated in the New Testament. The Ten Commandments, for example, still apply to us today.

The Old Testament did list a number of behaviors that were punishable by death. The Lord gave such harsh laws for Israel because they were the only country that worshipped the One, True God and they were called to live morally different lives from the pagans. Today, the same sins are still sin, but our civil consequences are not the same. Stealing is still a sin, but we don't cut off someone's hand because they stole something.

Adultery was listed in the Old Testament as a sin punishable by death; however, both the adulterer and the adulteress were to be put to death, as Leviticus 20:10 clearly states. The Pharisees were quick to drag the woman before Jesus, but not the man. Jesus pointed out their hypocrisy by reminding them they were just as sinful as the woman. "But what do you say?" they asked Him. At this point, Jesus stooped down and started writing something in the dirt. When He straightened up, He said in John 8:7, "If any one of you is without sin, let him be the first to throw a stone at her." Then He stooped down and wrote again. One by one, the people left.

Then, after they had all walked away, dropping their stones, Jesus turned to the woman and asked: " 'Woman, where are they? Has no one condemned you?' She replied, 'No one, sir,' to which He answered, 'Then neither do I condemn you. [. . .] Go now and leave your life of sin' " (John 8:10-11, NIV). Jesus is saying the same thing to you and me. He is calling us to leave our lifestyle and patterns of sin. He knows we will never be sinless this side of heaven; He is simply saying as we grow, we should be "sinning less".

What a beautiful story of our Lord's tender mercies toward us. Jesus upheld the law, He called adultery a sin. However, He taught an important life lesson to all in attendance. He said only the one with no sin could throw the first stone. He emphasized the truth that no one is without sin, and we all need forgiveness and mercy. I wonder, was he writing in the dirt the sins of those in attendance?

Jesus taught mercy by highlighting its relationship to judgment. Christians are often labeled judgmental, when we call certain behaviors sinful, because God's Word says they are sinful. Jesus never compromised the truth; what God called sin, He called sin. There's a place for judging. Judgment is the exercise of critical thinking. As Christians we have to make judgment calls that are discerning, wise, and truthful. However, we can so easily wade into the murky waters of sin by displaying a judgmental or critical spirit.

Check out what Jesus said in Matthew 7:1-5:

> "Do not judge others, and you will not be judged. For you will be treated as you treat others. The standard you use in judging is the standard by which you will be judged. And why worry about a speck in your friend's eye when you have a log in your own? How can you think of saying to your friend, 'Let me help you get rid of that speck in your eye,' when you can't see past the log in your own eye? Hypocrite! First get rid of the log in your own eye; then you will see well enough to deal with the speck in your friend's eye." (NLT)

What is the difference between making a judgment call and having a judgmental spirit?

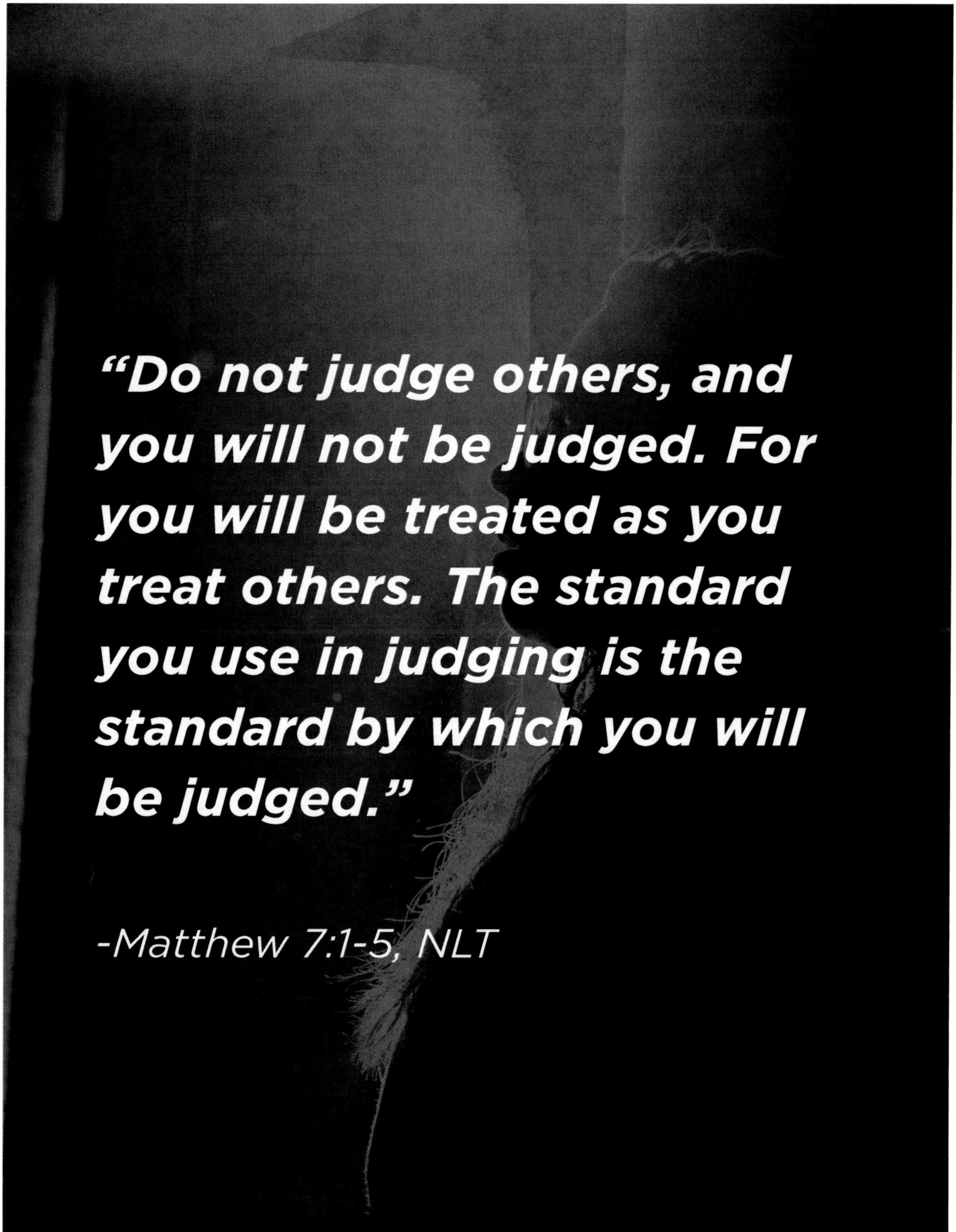
"Do not judge others, and you will not be judged. For you will be treated as you treat others. The standard you use in judging is the standard by which you will be judged."
-Matthew 7:1-5, NLT

day two

Before we unpack how having mercy is the opposite of having a judgmental, critical spirit, it is important to note that Jesus was not referring to four areas of relationships in the Matthew 7:1-5 passage. Note the areas to which he was NOT referring: parenting, teachers of God's Word, bosses at work and our country's legal system.

1. Parents are responsible to make judgment calls while raising their children. Discipline is used to correct and train people to go in the right way. Parents can't always show mercy. Mercy without rules leads to entitled, spoiled brats. However, as Josh McDowell teaches, "Rules without relationship, leads to rebellion." Parents have a difficult role in balancing judgment and mercy with their children. "No discipline seems pleasant at the time, but painful. Later on, however, it produces a harvest of righteousness and peace for those who have been trained by it." (Hebrews 12:11, NIV)

   But even while disciplining our children, we must always show mercy: "Fathers, do not provoke your children to anger [do not exasperate them to the point of resentment with demands that are trivial or unreasonable or humiliating or abusive; nor by showing favoritism or indifference to any of them], but bring them up [tenderly, with loving-kindness] in the discipline and instruction of the Lord." (Ephesians 6:4, AMP)

2. We have to make judgment calls with the pastors and teachers we follow. This does not mean we have a critical spirit; it simply means we are discerning.

   "Dear friends, do not believe everyone who claims to speak by the Spirit. You must test them to see if the spirit they have comes from God. For there are many false prophets in the world." (1 John 4:1, NLT)

How do we test teachers and pastors for truth? Ask the following questions:

What does this teacher say about Jesus? In Matthew 16:15-16, Jesus asks, "Who do you say I am?" Peter answers, "You are the Christ, the Son of the living God," and for this answer Peter is called "blessed."

"Who is the liar but the one who denies that Jesus is the Christ (the Messiah, the Anointed)? This is the antichrist [the enemy and antagonist of Christ], the one who denies and consistently refuses to acknowledge the Father and the Son." (1 John 2:22, AMP)

Does this teacher preach the gospel?

"All Scripture is God-breathed." (2 Timothy 3:16, NIV)

"I am shocked that you are turning away so soon from God, who called you to himself through the loving mercy of Christ. You are following a different way that pretends to be the Good News but is not the Good News at all. You are being fooled by those who deliberately twist the truth concerning Christ. Let God's curse fall on anyone, including us or even an angel from heaven, who preaches a different kind of Good News than the one we preached to you. (Galatians 1: 6-8, NLT)

Does this teacher exhibit character qualities that glorify the Lord?

"They have taken the way of Cain; they have rushed for profit into Balaam's error; they have been destroyed in Korah's rebellion." (Jude 11, NIV)

A false teacher can be known by his pride (Cain's rejection of God's plan), greed (Balaam's prophesying for money), and rebellion (Korah's promotion of himself over Moses). Jesus said to beware of such people and that we would know them by their fruits. (see Matthew 7:15-20)

It is often difficult to spot a false teacher/false prophet. "Satan masquerades as an angel of light . . ." (2 Corinthians 11:14), "and his ministers masquerade as servants of righteousness" (2 Corinthians 11:15a). Only by being thoroughly familiar with the truth will we be able to recognize a counterfeit.

3. Your boss at work. Your job is based on your performance. Your boss has the right to judge you, based on your work results. He or she is not obligated to show you mercy, when your performance does not measure up to the requirements expected of you.

4. Our legal system. The law is the law to keep order in our society and keep us safe. (see Romans 13).

   Matthew 7 illustrates Jesus' true intentions because He knows our bent is toward judgment and not mercy. However, it is impossible to enjoy the abundant life He promises us if we have a critical spirit toward others. We destroy what we all want most; we destroy relationships when we are judgmental and critical of others.

‣ Are you quick to see the gold in others or the dirt? Explain.

‣ Are you more likely to commend or condemn?

We can choose to see the good if we determine to do so.

We are all a combination of dirt and gold; we all have good and bad in us. Check out what Paul wrote: "You, therefore, have no excuse, you who pass judgment on someone else, for at whatever point you judge another, you are condemning yourself, because you who pass judgment do the same things" (Romans 2:1 NIV).

Self-awareness is important to our growth. When I am busy judging everyone around me, I can assure you I am not examining my own words and actions. Paul, led by the Holy Spirit of God, wrote these words to us: "But if we would examine ourselves, we would not be judged by God in this way" (1 Corinthians 11:31, NLT).

‣ Read this verse from Galatians. When are you most tempted to compare yourself with others?

Each person should judge his own actions and not compare himself with others. Then he can be proud for what he himself has done. (Galatians 6:4, NCV)

In 2 Chronicles 7:14 (NIV) God says, "If my people, who are called by my name, will humble themselves and pray and seek my face and turn from their wicked ways, then I will hear from heaven, and I will forgive their sin and will heal their land." Used here, the word for "pray" means to stop, meditate, and judge our own behavior. If we are seeking God's face after judging ourselves, we don't have the inclination to judge others.

This side of Glory we have work to do; we will never "arrive" in our walk with Jesus until we see Him face-to-face. In the meantime, Paul encourages us with these words:

I don't mean to say that I have already achieved these things or that I have already reached perfection. But I press on to possess that perfection for which Christ Jesus first possessed me. No, dear brothers and sisters, I have not achieved it, but I focus on this one thing: Forgetting the past and looking forward to what lies ahead, I press on to reach the end of the race and receive the heavenly prize for which God, through Christ Jesus, is calling us. (Philippians 3:12–14, NLT)

A great verse to pray for yourself as an antidote against judging others is this one:

Lord, please help me to get rid of all evil behavior. I want to be done with all deceit, hypocrisy, jealousy, and all unkind speech. Like a newborn baby, help me to crave pure spiritual milk so that I will grow into a full experience of salvation. I cry out for this nourishment, now that I have had a taste of Your mercy and kindness.

This personal prayer is adapted from 1 Peter 2:1-3 (NLT)

‣ Look at the verse again. Which of these do you struggle most with: deceit, hypocrisy, jealousy, or unkind speech?

‣ Where can you find "spiritual milk" to nourish your soul?

Confessing our struggle with sin is often the first step to overcoming a critical spirit.

daythree

As we discussed on day two, overcoming a critical spirit requires us to continually examine our own heart before the Lord, asking Him to reveal areas where we are falling short and need to grow. For me, this has been a humbling experience because He is so true to His promise that if we seek Him, we will find Him. He has opened my eyes daily to His bountiful mercies in my life. The amazing thing about being honest and reflective before the Lord is how merciful He is, when He does point out our sin to us. His goal is never to make us feel bad about ourselves, but rather to grow us closer to Him and to transform us more into His glorious image. Mercy!

Notice that Jesus didn't say we never need to deal with issues that arise with others. He said don't be a self-righteous hypocrite, and make sure you are not living in any pattern of sin while pointing out the sin of others. We have to make sure we are not tangled up in any strongholds of repeated sin before approaching someone else's shortcomings. Jesus said,"Hypocrite! First get rid of the log in your own eye; then you will see well enough to deal with the speck in your friend's eye" (Matthew 7:5, NLT).

Life includes relationships, and part of having healthy relationships is the need to occasionally confront with care. We are not permitted to have judgmental spirits, but we are called within our relationships to make judgment calls and speak truth with love. Sometimes not speaking up demonstrates a lack of concern or love for another.

Paul warns us our goal is always to restore, not to destroy. He says, "Dear brothers and sisters, if another believer is overcome by some sin, you who are godly should gently and humbly help that person back onto the right path. And be careful not to fall into the same temptation yourself" (Galatians 6:1, NLT).

Paul warns us to be careful because someday the person falling into the same temptation could be you. Hopefully, a godly soul will come alongside you and nudge you back on track with gentleness and mercy.

Christians must judge or discern between truth and lies, good and evil. How do we become discerning? I love this translation of Proverbs 4:20-22 from The Message: "Dear friend, listen well to my words; tune your ears to my voice. Keep my message in plain view at all times. Concentrate! Learn it by heart! Those who discover these words live, really live; body and soul, they're bursting with health."

Abba Father wants His children to have well informed opinions rooted in His truths; not what we think or feel. He wants us to be discerning and to make good judgment calls. In fact, immediately after Jesus warned His disciples against hypocritical judgment, He said, "Do not give dogs what is holy, and do not throw your pearls before pigs." (Matthew 7:6, NIV)

In other words, don't share God's treasures of truth with someone who has absolutely zero interest in them.

How are we supposed to know who the "dogs" and the "pigs" are unless we exercise wisdom and discernment?

Wisdom is a mark of growing and maturing in Christ. Wisdom always considers how best to speak the truth with love and mercy. If we are not wise, we blurt out truth without caring for the other person, leaving a trail of collateral damage. Those who do this will often defend their words by pointing out they were true, but in reality they are demonstrating their lack of maturity and mercy.

‣Read Ephesians 4:15 (NIV): Instead, speaking the truth in love, we will grow to become in every respect the mature body of Him who is the head, that is, Christ. What does it mean to speak the truth in love? What promise do you find in this verse?

Iron sharpens iron, as Scripture says, and if I see my brother or sister going off a spiritual or moral cliff, it is my responsibility to lovingly confront them. "My dear brothers and sisters, if someone among you wanders away from the truth and is brought back, you can be sure that whoever brings the sinner back from wandering will save that person from death and bring about the forgiveness of many sins." (James 5:19-20, NLT) James ended his letter with a call for mercy. He was concerned about believers living in patterns of sin and not living in obedience to God. The death he is most likely referring to is the quenching of the Spirit within us because of moral corruption. This of course results in spiritual emptiness and unhappiness, rather than the abundant life God promises His children.

›How can you confront with great care?

›What does it look like to honor the Lord when we confront another?

day four

If we feel God is calling us to confront another, Scripture is clear about how we do that and honor our Lord at the same time. We confront with mercy. But first, I must ask myself if I am taking any pleasure and satisfaction in pointing out the sin. If I am, then I should not be confronting. Jesus grieved over sin:

"As he came closer to Jerusalem and saw the city ahead, he began to weep. 'How I wish today that you of all people would understand the way to peace. But now it is too late, and peace is hidden from your eyes'" (Luke 19:41-42, NLT).

Never judge anyone until you have grieved for them.

The word for "weep" used in this verse implies wailing. Jesus didn't just shed a passing tear for Jerusalem. He grieved deeply for the people. If you don't care enough about the person to be deeply grieved for them in their sin, then you should not be confronting them about any speck of sin in their life.

Second, we should ask: Am I willing to invest my time in order to restore the person I'm confronting to spiritual health?

God's desire in pointing out our sin is always motivated by the hope of restoring our relationship to Him. This is mercy. Mercy takes action in order to make someone's life better. To be judgmental is to rejoice in pointing out sin and then to refuse to reach out to the sinner (investing time in them) to restore him or her to spiritual health. Before you point out any specks in others' lives, you must ask yourself, "Do I truly want the very best for this person?"

Investing in someone sends the message that although you may disagree with them, you accept them. Jesus accepted everyone who came to Him, even if He did not approve of their choices. In fact, the Holy Spirit of God wrote through Paul, "Accept each other just as Christ has accepted you so that God will be given glory" (Romans 15:7, NLT).

▸ How can we demonstrate that we accept others without agreeing with, or approving of their choices?

___

___

___

When we love others—our greatest commandment for goodness sake!—we are truly walking our walk as believers. Accepting others by investing in them is simply being kind, gentle, considerate, patient, generous, willing to share, and forgiving. The way I treat others is a reflection of who I am in Christ, regardless of how they treat me. Pastor Rick Warren says, "Love is not saying I approve of everything you do. Love is saying I accept you in spite of what you do."

And I would add that loving someone says you matter just because you are a human, no matter where you have been or how you are currently living.

Warren, Rick. Online Daily Devotional. June 29, 2016. *Acceptance Does Not Require Approval.* Copyright 2017

‣Spend a little time in prayer asking God to show you the truth about any critical, judgmental spirit that is in your heart. You may want to use the following to guide your prayer Time.

Dear *Abba* Father, thank You for showing me mercy in my life. Lord, I ask that You open the eyes of my heart, when I criticize or judge without love. I ask that any judgmental words I use would feel like heavy mud in my mouth. Thank You that You are a Lord who desires to set me free to live the abundant, fruitful, joyful, hopeful and peaceful life you designed for me. I am sorry for thinking I am better than others. Please forgive me. Open my eyes every day to Your mercies that are new for me every morning. Thank You, for great is Your faithfulness. In Jesus' Name, Amen.

Finally, remember that ultimately the issue is not seeking to get people to change their behavior, but for them to come to know and believe in Christ. We cannot change anyone; only Jesus can bring about change. Only He can set a person free from the law of sin and death (Romans 3:2). Our job is to love, speak the truth with incredible care, and show mercy. "There will be no mercy for those who have not shown mercy to others. But if you have been merciful, God will be merciful when he judges you" (James 2:13, NLT.) Or as the NIV translates this: "mercy triumphs over judgment."

‣What new mercy did you receive from God today?

‣What is your role in other people's lives?

video TEACHING WEEK 2

The Merciful do not have a judgmental Spirit

"Do not judge others, and you will not be judged. For you will be treated as you treat others. The standard you use in judging others is the standard by which you will be judged." (Matthew 7: 1-5)

What situations tend to bring out your judgmental spirit?

____

____

____

Practical steps to resist having a critical or judgmental spirit:

1. Walk with God. We must choose to walk with Him under the control of the ____________ ____________ rather than the control of the ____________________.

2. Know yourself. Finding faults in ____________________ keeps us from dealing with our own _____________ and ________________.

   Comparing ourselves with others often leads to ____________________ that cause a ____________________ attitude.

3. Build others up.. When we have a right-sized view of _____________, we can be

   ______________ to _____________ and build up others.

   "Don't copy the behavior and customs of this world, but let God transform you into a new person by changing the way you think. Then you will learn to know God's will for you, which is good and pleasing and perfect." (Romans 12:2)

   Four ways to deal with conflict without having a critical spirit:

   1) Use ____ statements. Avoid _________ words like "you always" or "you never."

   2) Engage with _________________. Ask the ______________________ to help you.

   3) Examine your ________________. Ask: Am I taking any __________________ and

   ________________ in pointing out the sin in another?

   4) Invest in ________________. Ask: Am I willing to invest my ______________ in order to

   _______________ this person to spiritual health?

WEEK three

THE MERCIFUL LOVE THEIR ENEMIES

Day one is a bit long, but it is worth it! The story of Jonah sets the stage for this week's study on mercy. Find a comfy place and bless yourself with these ancient words of wisdom.

Jonah Runs from the Lord

The Lord gave this message to Jonah son of Amittai: "Get up and go to the great city of Nineveh. Announce my judgment against it because I have seen how wicked its people are." But Jonah got up and went in the opposite direction to get away from the Lord. He went down to the port of Joppa, where he found a ship leaving for Tarshish. He bought a ticket and went on board, hoping to escape from the Lord by sailing to Tarshish. But the Lord hurled a powerful wind over the sea, causing a violent storm that threatened to break the ship apart. . . . "Throw me into the sea," Jonah said, "and it will become calm again. I know that this terrible storm is all my fault." Instead, the sailors rowed even harder to get the ship to the land. But the stormy sea was too violent for them, and they couldn't make it. Then they cried out to the Lord, Jonah's God. "O Lord," they pleaded, "don't make us die for this man's sin. And don't hold us responsible for his death. O Lord, you have sent this storm upon him for your own good reasons."

Then the sailors picked Jonah up and threw him into the raging sea, and the storm stopped at once! The sailors were awestruck by the Lord's great power, and they offered him a sacrifice and vowed to serve him.

Taken from Jonah 1, NLT

Jonah's Prayer

"Then Jonah prayed to the Lord his God from inside the fish. He said, "I cried out to the Lord in my great trouble, and He answered me. I called to you from the land of the dead, and Lord, you heard me! As my life was slipping away, I remembered the Lord. And my earnest prayer went out to you in your holy Temple. Those who worship false gods turn their backs on all God's mercies. But I will offer sacrifices to you with songs of praise, and I will fulfill all my vows. For my salvation comes from the Lord alone" (taken from Jonah 2 NLT).

Jonah Goes to Nineveh

Then the Lord spoke to Jonah a second time, "Get up and go to the great city of Nineveh, and deliver the message I have given you." This time Jonah obeyed the Lord's command and went to Nineveh, a city so large that it took three days to see it all. On the day Jonah entered the city, he shouted to the crowds: "Forty days from now Nineveh will be destroyed!" The people of Nineveh believed God's message, and from the greatest to the least, they declared a fast and put on burlap to show their sorrow.

When the king of Nineveh heard what Jonah was saying, he stepped down from his throne and took off his royal robes. He dressed himself in burlap and sat on a heap of ashes. Then the king and his nobles sent this decree throughout the city,

"No one, not even the animals from your herds and flocks, may eat or drink anything at all. People and animals alike must wear garments of mourning, and everyone must pray earnestly to God. They must turn from their evil ways and stop all their violence. Who can tell? Perhaps even yet God will change his mind and hold back his fierce anger from destroying us."

When God saw what they had done and how they had put a stop to their evil ways, he changed his mind and did not carry out the destruction he had threatened." (Jonah 3, NLT).

Jonah's Anger at the Lord's Mercy

This change of plans greatly upset Jonah, and he became very angry. So he complained to the Lord, "Didn't I say before I left home that you would do this, Lord? That is why I ran away to Tarshish! I knew that you are a merciful and compassionate God, slow to get angry and filled with unfailing love. You are eager to turn back from destroying people. Just kill me now, Lord! I'd rather be dead than alive if what I predicted will not happen."

The Lord replied, "Is it right for you to be angry about this?"

Then Jonah went out to the east side of the city and made a shelter to sit under as he waited to see what would happen to the city. And the Lord God arranged for a leafy plant to grow there, and soon it spread its broad leaves over Jonah's head, shading him from the sun. This eased his discomfort, and Jonah was very grateful for the plant. But God also arranged for a worm! The next morning at dawn the worm ate through the stem of the plant so that it withered away. And as the sun grew hot, God arranged for a scorching east wind to blow on Jonah. The sun beat down on his head until he grew faint and wished to die. "Death is certainly better than living like this!" he exclaimed.

Then God said to Jonah, "Is it right for you to be angry because the plant died?"

"Yes," Jonah retorted, "even angry enough to die!"

Then the Lord said, "You feel sorry about the plant, though you did nothing to put it there. It came quickly and died quickly. But Nineveh has more than 120,000 people living in spiritual darkness, not to mention all the animals. Shouldn't I feel sorry for such a great city?" (Jonah 4, NLT).

Jonah was written between 800 and 750 BC, before Israel was conquered by Assyria forty years later in 722 BC. Centered on the Tigris River, the Assyrian Empire covered modern northern Iraq, northeastern Syria, southeastern Turkey and parts of northwestern Iran.

A legal code from the 13th and 14th centuries showed, among other things, that Assyria, had much harsher laws than most of the region. The social position of women in Assyria was lower than that of neighboring societies. Executions, severe beatings, mutilations, and other forms of suffering were not uncommon in Assyrian society. Women were dealt with especially harshly. Assyria was a hated and cruel nation. The Assyrians tortured their prisoners of war by tearing the skin from their bodies and then leaving them to die in the sweltering hot sun. They did not value human life like the Israelites did, and they were known to torture children they captured before executing them.

Also, unlike the Israelites, they not only practiced depraved cruelty, they celebrated it and built monuments to proclaim their evil ways. As you can imagine, in Jonah's mind, to bless them was to curse Israel.

Jonah was my kind of guy; he loved his God and he loved his country. Jonah's ministry in the Northern kingdom of Israel was during King Jeroboam II's reign, and although King Jeroboam worshipped false gods, he did listen to Jonah on some accounts.

"He was the one who restored the boundaries of Israel from Lebo Hamath to the Dead Sea, in accordance with the word of the LORD, the God of Israel, spoken through his servant Jonah son of Amittai, the prophet from Gath Hepher." (2 Kings 14:25, NIV)

Jonah had favor with God and the ear of his King. He was greatly loved by God, and his call as a prophet of God was to share that love with others. The Lord is Lord of all. God has a merciful love for all. Jonah had no problem sharing his Lord with his beloved countrymen, but he had zero interest in the evil Assyrians receiving any mercy and love from the Lord.

Why didn't Jonah want the cruel Assyrians to experience mercy?

Jonah did not want the evil Assyrians to experience God's mercy because he felt they certainly did not deserve mercy. I can't help but think how I might struggle, if the Lord asked me to share a message of mercy with ISIS. Every day Christians are being slaughtered in the Middle East by ISIS in the same region where the Assyrians once ruled. The Christian population in Iraq has dropped by 82%–that's over one million displaced or slaughtered. The ISIS genocide continues.

In a 2014 New York Times article, Who Will Stand Up for the Christians? author Ronald S. Lauder, asks: "WHY is the world silent, while Christians are being slaughtered in the Middle East and Africa? The Middle East and parts of central Africa are losing entire Christian communities that have lived in peace for centuries. Half a million Christian Arabs have been driven out of Syria, and Christians have been persecuted and killed in countries from Lebanon to Sudan"

"The Islamic State in Iraq and Syria (ISIS) is not a loose coalition of jihadist groups but a real military force that has managed to take over much of Iraq. It uses money from banks and gold shops it has captured, along with control of oil resources, to finance its killing machine, making it perhaps the wealthiest Islamist terrorist group in the world. But where it truly excels is in its carnage, rivaling the death orgies of the Middle Ages. It has ruthlessly targeted Shiites, Kurds and Christians."

"They actually behead children and put their heads on a stick!" a Chaldean-American businessman named Mark Arabo told CNN, describing a scene in a Mosul park. "More children are getting beheaded, mothers are getting raped and killed, and fathers are being hung."

At the time of this article's publication, 200,000 Aramaeans had fled their ancestral homeland around Nineveh, having already escaped Mosul. And not mentioned in this article were the many children crucified by ISIS, when they would not deny Jesus as their Lord and Savior.

I can imagine how Jonah felt, when the Lord asked him to visit Israel's enemy and share a message of repentance leading to mercy. The Assyrians were a constant terror and threat to the people of Israel, and God wanted Jonah to preach a message that might save their souls. "No way," thought Jonah, and he went to the port of Joppa and got on the first ship heading to Spain, the exact opposite direction of Assyria!

Jonah ran away, but Abba stayed with His runaway because our Abba Father is ever so merciful. Even when we are disobedient, God is committed to His children.

‣ Please look up Romans 5:8-10. How did God demonstrate mercy toward us?

Ronald S. Lauder, The New York Times, August 19, 2014. *Who Will Stand Up for the Christians?*

Please look up Matthew 18:12-14. Based on this verse, list three words that describe the character of God and His love.

The Lord heard Jonah and delivered him; Abba showed mercy by taking action to save Jonah. The mercy Jonah experienced was the mercy he was called to preach to Nineveh (Jonah 3:1, NIV)

Don't you love this demonstration of God's mercy toward Jonah? Jonah cried out, and God went running to his side. Jonah knew better and yet he disobeyed, but when he repented, God heard him and forgave him immediately. Jonah may have thought his direct disobedience meant his ministry was over, but the Lord gave him a second chance and told him to get moving. Don't ever think the Lord is finished with you! If you are alive and breathing, God has plans for you.

Have you ever thought that you did something that might cause the Lord to never use you for His glory?

Do you believe that the heart of God is to forgive AND to restore when we repent?

It took Jonah three days to walk through the entire city of Nineveh, shouting out to the people, "Forty more days and Nineveh will be destroyed." To Jonah's shock and disappointment the wicked people were convicted, repented, fasted, and believed God. Jonah 3 tells us God showed them mercy and did not bring destruction upon them.

"Jonah would later write when reflecting on being in the belly of the great fish: "When my life was ebbing away, I remembered you, Lord, and my prayer rose to You, to Your holy temple." (Jonah 2:7, NIV).

Mercy! God's Mercy is greater than any sin we can ever commit. Abba always welcomes with open arms any person or nation who repents and turns to Him. The heart of God is for us to be reconciled to Him; for us to be in a relationship with Him. Can you give Him a big ol' THANK YOU?!!

day three

What pleased God (Jonah 3:10) greatly angered Jonah. That God's wrath had been averted by His merciful response to Nineveh's repentance made Jonah angry. God didn't do what Jonah wanted God to do with Nineveh, so he sank into self-pity and asked God to let him die! He didn't want Nineveh to experience the very same mercy God showed to him. Yes, he did obey God and share His message of mercy, but he did it with a bad attitude. His heart was not right with God, nor with his enemy. Jonah was a good prophet in Israel and had mercy for "his people," but he wished only destruction and judgment for his enemies. God didn't want Jonah to just obey Him; Abba Father desires our hearts to be in step with His heart. And His heart is one of great mercy! His heart gives 10,000 mercies to one judgment!

‣ Think of a time when you obeyed God but had an ungodly attitude. What factors impacted your attitude?

‣ What do you think God wants you to do when this happens?

There are no more striking examples of God's unconditional mercy within us than to show mercy to an enemy or someone who doesn't even acknowledge our help. When we are merciful, we are motivated to help and serve in order to meet needs, not from what we get out of it; this is unconditional mercy. Consider Jesus' teaching on this topic:

"But to you who are listening I say: Love your enemies, do good to those who hate you, bless those who curse you, pray for those who mistreat you. If someone slaps you on one cheek, turn to them the other also. If someone takes your coat, do not withhold your shirt from them. Give to everyone who asks you, and if anyone takes what belongs to you, do not demand it back. Do to others as you would have them do to you.

If you love those who love you, what credit is that to you? Even sinners love those who love them. And if you do good to those who are good to you, what credit is that to you? Even sinners do that. And if you lend to those from whom you expect repayment, what credit is that to you? Even sinners lend to sinners, expecting to be repaid in full. But love your enemies, do good to them, and lend to them without expecting to get anything back. Then your reward will be great, and you will be children of the Most High, because he is kind to the ungrateful and wicked. Be merciful, just as your Father is merciful (Luke 6:27-36, NIV).

Showing mercy when I get nothing in return is not about them; it is about my heart. It is always about where my heart is with Jesus.

▸How do most people treat their enemies?

▸Do you think it is possible to show mercy to our enemies without Jesus in our hearts? Explain.

▸Why would Abba ask us to show mercy to our enemies?

Mercifully for Jonah, God did not answer his prayer to die. Instead God responded in great kindness and tenderness rather than judgment. He asked Jonah to ponder and reflect on whether he had good reason to be angry. God encouraged Jonah to self-reflect, to examine his heart. Remember our verse from last week, "But if we would examine ourselves, we would not be judged by God in this way." (1 Corinthians 11:31, NLT)

Jonah sat in hope for Nineveh to return to wickedness that would result in their judgment. Jonah wanted circumstances to change, but God was seeking to ignite a change in Jonah's heart.

▸Think about a time you prayed for your circumstances to change. What happened?

▸Think about a time the Lord changed your heart instead of your circumstances. How would you describe the change that occurred in your heart in that situation?

The Book of Jonah ends with the Lord saying to Jonah, "You feel sorry about the plant, though you did nothing to put it there. It came quickly and died quickly. But Nineveh has more than 120,000 people living in spiritual darkness, not to mention all the animals. Shouldn't I feel sorry for such a great city?" (Jonah 4:10-11, NLT)

Nineveh was filled with eternal beings whom God loved. Self-preoccupation such as Jonah's can be as blinding as the glaring sun he was sitting under. Often, being preoccupied with my own comforts and wants leads to valuing temporal comforts over God's will and the souls of men and women. Jonah was focused on a plant that shaded him from the scorching, blistering sun and didn't seem to care that these souls were headed for an eternity of hell and discomfort.

"The Lord isn't really being slow about his promise, as some people think. No, he is being patient for your sake. He does not want anyone to be destroyed, but wants everyone to repent." (2 Peter 3:9, NLT) Every person comes from the Hand of God. We are all made in the image of God; however, He leaves the choice up to us whether we will be His children and part of His eternal family.

God's question ends the book of Jonah in order to help us learn about God's mercy. He is merciful. He desires that His people obey Him and not put limits on His love and mercy. God is kind to evil and ungrateful people (MERCY!) and patiently desires repentance.

God's mercy, like God's love, does not have strings attached–it is unconditional. But Jesus did attach a promise to His exhortation in Luke 6 for us to love our enemies, He said, "Your reward will be great, and you will be sons and daughters of the Most High." God does notice when we reflect His Mercy to the world.

When I show mercy to the undeserving, especially my enemies, it doesn't reflect their character, it reflects my character in Jesus Christ.

▸Who is your enemy? Who popped into your head when doing this lesson?

▸Whom is the Lord asking you to show mercy to today? Remember mercy is an action, not just an emotion. What action can you take to show mercy?

video TEACHING WEEK 3

"You have heard the law that says, 'Love your neighbor and hate your enemy'. But I say, love your enemies! Pray for those who persecute you! In that way, you will be acting as true children of your Father in heaven. For he gives his sunlight to both the evil and the good, and he sends rain on the just and the unjust alike." (Matthew 5:43-45)

Three spiritual practices that have helped me to begin to show mercy to my enemies:

1) __________________ for them. _________________ means we have the ability to step back and focus more on the _________________ than the ______________ they inflicted.

2) ___________________ our enemy.

3) Be __________________ with our enemy. Loving your enemy means offering your ______________ with the ______________ things in life.

"If your enemy is hungry, feed him, and if he is thirsty, give him a drink." (Romans 12:20)

These things are not easy. But if we ask God, He will help us to not only do these things, but to have the ______________ to show mercy to our enemies. HE can _________________ our hearts.

The Bible encourages us to press on. Why?

1) God uses every little thing for ______________ ______________.

2) We are going to __________________ a ________________.

"Blessed are you when men or women cast insults at you, and persecute you, and say all kinds of evil against you falsely, on account of Me. Rejoice, and be glad, for your reward in heaven is great, for so they persecuted the prophets who were before you." (Matthew 5:11-12)

WEEK

four

THE MERCIFUL RECEIVE AND OFFER FORGIVENESS

"Save me, O God, for the floodwaters are up to my neck. Deeper and deeper I sink into the mire; I can't find a foothold. I am in deep water, and the floods overwhelm me. I am exhausted from crying for help; my throat is parched. My eyes are swollen with weeping, waiting for my God to help me. Those who hate me without cause outnumber the hairs on my head. Many enemies try to destroy me with lies, demanding that I give back what I didn't steal."

Psalm 69:1-4, NLT

In the last session, we discussed how the Lord calls us to show mercy to our enemies, which leads us into this session regarding forgiveness. King David demonstrated incredible mercy toward his enemies and worked hard to have a heart of forgiveness toward them.

For eight years Saul pursued David, who had done nothing to stir up Saul's hatred toward him. Saul had a spirit of jealousy, one of the most dangerous sins because it leads one to have a hard, bitter heart toward others. Saul relentlessly pursued David with an intent to harm him and even tried to kill him on several occasions. And yet, David mourned and wept when he heard of Saul's demise.

Then David and all the men with him took hold of their clothes and tore them. They mourned and wept and fasted till evening for Saul and his son Jonathan, and for the army of the Lord and for the nation of Israel, because they had fallen by the sword. (2 Samuel 1:11-12, NIV)

David demonstrated his heart of mercy further by reaching out to Saul's grandson. Remember, mercy is not all talk. Mercy takes action to make someone's life better.

Now there was a servant of Saul's household named Ziba. They summoned him to appear before David, and the king said to him, "Are you Ziba?" "At your service," he replied. The king asked, "Is there no one still alive from the house of Saul to whom I can show God's kindness?" Ziba answered the king, "There is still a son of Jonathan; he is lame in both feet."

When Mephibosheth son of Jonathan, the son of Saul, came to David, he bowed down to pay him honor. David said, "Mephibosheth!" "At your service," he replied. "Don't be afraid," David said to him, "for I will surely show you kindness for the sake of your father Jonathan. I will restore to you all the land that belonged to your grandfather Saul, and you will always eat at my table." Mephibosheth bowed down and said, "What is your servant, that you should notice a dead dog like me?"

Then the king summoned Ziba, Saul's steward, and said to him, "I have given your master's grandson everything that belonged to Saul and his family. You and your sons and your servants are to farm the land for him and bring in the crops, so that your master's grandson may be provided for. And Mephibosheth, grandson of your master, will always eat at my table." (Now Ziba had fifteen sons and twenty servants.)

So Mephibosheth ate at David's table like one of the king's sons. Mephibosheth had a young son named Mika, and all the members of Ziba's household were servants of Mephibosheth. And Mephibosheth lived in Jerusalem, because he always ate at the king's table; he was lame in both feet. (2 Samuel 9:2-13, NIV)

Mephibosheth had every reason to fear when summoned before King David. It was customary in that day to kill the sons and grandsons of your enemies because they most likely would grow up with plans to revenge their lost loved ones. Not only did David demonstrate a heart of forgiveness, but by inviting Saul's grandson to sit at his table with his family, David also demonstrated mercy when it was not expected. Mercy requires action to make someone's life better, and mercy forfeits the right to be angry, offended or to get even. Mercy forgives.

▸ Who is God quickening your heart to show mercy toward by forgiving them?

day two

Parable of the Unforgiving Debtor

Then Peter came to him and asked, "Lord, how often should I forgive someone who sins against me? Seven times?" (Matthew 18:21)

Jewish tradition would forgive three times, so Peter doubled the number and added another one for good measure.

"No, not seven times," Jesus replied, "but seventy times seven!"

Jesus was saying so many times you don't keep track of how many times. He told a parable to illustrate his teaching on forgiveness.

Therefore, the kingdom of heaven is like a king who wanted to settle accounts with his servants. As he began the settlement, a man who owed him ten thousand bags of gold [millions of dollars that the servant could not possibly repay] was brought to him. Since he was not able to pay, the master ordered that he and his wife and his children and all that he had be sold to repay the debt.

At this the servant fell on his knees before him. 'Be patient with me,' he begged, 'and I will pay back everything.' The servant's master took pity on him, cancelled the debt and let him go.

This would be like having your car payment cancelled, your credit card debt cancelled, your mortgage, and student loans cancelled!

▸How would you feel if you received such mercy? This is the measure of mercy our Master, Jesus, shows us every day. In what ways have you experienced God's mercy in your life?

But when that servant went out, he found one of his fellow servants who owed him a hundred silver coins. He grabbed him and began to choke him. 'Pay back what you owe me!' he demanded. "His fellow servant fell to his knees and begged him, 'Be patient with me, and I will pay it back.' "But he refused. Instead, he went off and had the man thrown into prison until he could pay the debt. When the other servants saw what had happened, they were outraged and went and told their master everything that had happened.

Even though the one who was blessed didn't see God's mercy, everyone around him seemed to recognize how Merciful his master was with him.

▸Why do you think we can see the mercy God offers others more easily than we can see His mercy in our own lives?

Then the master called the servant in. 'You wicked servant,' he said, 'I cancelled all that debt of yours because you begged me to. Shouldn't you have had mercy on your fellow servant just as I had on you?' In anger his master handed him over to the jailers to be tortured, until he should pay back all he owed.

This is how my heavenly Father will treat each of you unless you forgive your brother or sister from your heart. (Matthew 18:21-35, NLT)

Abba Father is serious about His daughters and sons practicing mercy and forgiveness. His motive is always for our best; He wants us to live in freedom and enjoy the spiritually and emotionally abundant life He designed for us. We are not living in freedom if bitter roots are wrapped around our emotional hearts and clogging up our thinking. Remember, just because we have a new Spirit living inside of us, we do not automatically receive a new emotionally clean heart or a new way of thinking. This happens over time, when we continually choose His ways. This is called the sanctification process.

Abba showers us with His mercy and forgiveness every day, but we must choose to recognize His mercy in our lives. The wicked servant didn't have a heart to forgive his fellow servant because he didn't have eyes to see his master's mercy and forgiveness in his life. He didn't have eyes to see the master's mercy. Do you see God's mercy in your life every day? God cancels our debts every day!

You are a God of forgiveness, always ready to pardon, gracious and merciful, slow to become angry, and full of love and MERCY. (Nehemiah 9:17b, TLB)

▸Look up Colossians 2:13-14. What do you think it means to be made alive in Christ?

▸What is your response to Abba Father's forgiveness of ALL your sins?

▸What does it mean to you that God has nailed your offenses to the cross of Jesus?

In order to fully receive His mercy and forgiveness, we need to understand two things about forgiveness:

First, we can never be good enough or do enough to earn or buy forgiveness.

Therefore, my friends, I want you to know that through Jesus the forgiveness of sins is proclaimed to you. (Acts 13:38, NIV)

The word "forgive" means to wipe clean or to cancel a debt. You and I do not have the power to scrub our souls white as snow or wipe away our debts. We are just not that good or powerful. But because God created us, loves us, and desires to be in a close relationship with us, He stands ready to forgive us of every sin and offense.

He grants us forgiveness, but not because we ever deserve it. No one deserves forgiveness. He grants us forgiveness because of His mercy toward us. He forgives you and me, despite what we do to offend Him. As the Bible reminds us, "Not a single person on earth is always good and never sins" (Ecclesiastes 7:20, NLT).

All sin is rebellion against God. "I did what you said is wrong. You are the one I have sinned against. I say this so that people will know that I am wrong and you are right. What you decided is fair." (Psalm 51:4, ERV) Our inner being, our souls, so desperately need to call sin out and ask for God's forgiveness and then receive His forgiveness and say "Thank You, Lord!" Forgiveness is not for sale, Jesus is not for sale, and we cheapen His gift of forgiveness, when we try to earn it. Thankfully, we don't need to earn God's favor or forgiveness. It is ours to accept and receive: "In Him we have redemption through His blood, the forgiveness of sins, in accordance with the riches of God's grace" (Ephesians 1:7, NIV).

Additionally, if we have a personal relationship with Jesus Christ, then all the forgiveness we will ever need already belongs to us; we must choose to push away our unbelief and our lack of understanding and doubts . . . and receive His forgiveness.

Forgiveness—is it really that easy? Yes it is that easy! You can't earn forgiveness from God. You can't pay for your forgiveness from God. You can only receive it, by faith, through the grace and mercy of God. You can only say, "I believe You Lord, and I receive Your forgiveness." Have you chosen to receive God's mercy and forgiveness over you?

One way you know you have done so is that you don't walk around with lingering guilt. Guilt is helpful when we feel that little check in our spirit; the Holy Spirit is telling us we are guilty of sin and inviting us to repent. But once we repent, God immediately forgives us, no waiting period, no thinking it over.

Done. Forgiven.

Guilt is like a red warning light in your car. My red warning light was on recently because one of my tires needed air. I didn't keep driving on a low tire, but instead I did something about it. I fixed the tire. I could have had an accident if I hadn't fixed that tire. We can so easily wreck our lives when we ignore the warning signs.

After I chose to have the tire fixed, the red light went off. I don't get into my car and stare where the warning light once was; I move forward in confidence, knowing the problem was addressed. And once you and I choose to repent of our sin, we needn't dwell on our past mistakes. If the sin comes to mind, don't allow the enemy to condemn you and play that tape over and over! Instead say, "Thank You Lord, You already took care of that for me."

▸ Have you ever chosen to believe in His promise of forgiveness? What appeals to you about saying, "I trust You, Jesus, and believe in You?"

I hope you will say, "Thank You, Jesus, that Your blood washes me as clean as freshly fallen snow. Thank You for Your mercy and forgiveness. Yes, I do choose to believe You and receive forgiveness. Thank You that your mercy is greater than any sin I ever committed or will commit.",

Choosing to accept God's mercy and forgiveness is not only critical for our transformation in Christ, it is also critical for living the abundant life of freedom in Christ. It is critical because you and I cannot give someone something we have not chosen to receive. Forgiveness is a two-way street; you and I cannot receive what we are unwilling to give.

If you forgive those who sin against you, your heavenly Father will forgive you. But if you refuse to forgive others, your Father will not forgive your sins. (Matthew 6:14-15, NLT)

We need forgiveness on an ongoing basis; this side of glory we will never be sinless. There will always be sin in our lives and in the lives of others. Therefore, we need to live in a circle of forgiveness; constantly seeking it, receiving it, and offering it. If we don't live this lifestyle, we will NOT be healthy Christians. How much forgiveness do those in the world offer? As Christians we are called to reflect Christ, the constant forgiver!

Forgiveness is not easy. Abba Father knows how hard it is, so His Word gives us some great direction to follow. These steps work:

STEP 1

Don't confuse petty offenses with deep wounds. Try to keep offenses in perspective, especially within our families. People get tired, grumpy, stressed and sick and sometimes hurtful words are spoken against us. Show some mercy toward someone having a bad day. We all say things we regret.

It is to one's glory to overlook an offense. (Proverbs 19:11b NIV)

Love forgets mistakes; nagging about them parts the best of friends. (Proverbs 17:9 TLB)

The more of God's love I allow in my heart, the harder it is for me to be offended. If I am filled with God's love, I am not so affected by others' bad behavior.

▸ What do you think it means to have a tough hide and tender heart? How can you develop both?

____

____

____

STEP 2

Pray for the offender. Forgiveness is required when you have been wounded. Unlike careless offenses, deep wounds cause great pain. If we don't deal with the pain God's way, it will turn to bitterness. We don't want bitter hearts that lead to bitter, unfruitful, empty lives.

Take your pain to the mighty throne of mercy! Determine to pray for the offender. Ask God to bless them with His truth and mercy. Ask God to bring them to repentance. Ask God to bless them with His presence and peace. Ask God to keep your heart soft toward them, and thank Him for always forgiving you. Repeat this prayer as long as it takes to feel it. Sometimes it takes a while for our hearts to catch up with our choice to obey God.

Bless those who curse you. Pray for those who hurt you. (Luke 6:28, NLT)

▸ Who has hurt you? How should you pray for them?

____

____

____

STEP 3

Trust Jesus to deal with the offender. Determine from the beginning that you are trusting the Lord with this wound. Keep saying, "I trust You, Jesus. This hurt did not slip by You, and You have got this" He sees all the extenuating circumstances. We can trust Him to take care of the offender much better than you and I can.

Dear friends, never take revenge. Leave that to the righteous anger of God. For the Scriptures say, "I will take revenge; I will pay them back," says the Lord. (Romans 12:19, NLT)

▸What specific situation are you facing right now where you want to take revenge? Spend some time in prayer, affirming your trust in the Lord to deal with your offender.

____

____

____

STEP 4

Forgive no matter what the other person does, or does not do, to acknowledge their sinful behavior. Forgiveness, like mercy, is unconditional. We don't attach strings to our forgiveness. Forgiveness is not dependent on anything the offender does or does not do to seek forgiveness. Forgiveness is dependent on my heart of mercy; it is my choice to forgive.

I recently had a situation where a church leader deeply wounded me. He believed someone who

had slandered me, and then he in turn slandered me and said untrue things about me. I felt the Holy Spirit encourage me to fully forgive him because he was misled. Of course, Jesus is our example of unbelievable forgiveness. He was in such agony nailed to a cross, as He looked down upon those who unjustly accused Him and prayed, "Father, forgive them, for they don't know what they are doing." (Luke 23:34, NLT)

Did His accusers ask for forgiveness? Did they say they were sorry? Did they say they would never do it again? Did they deserve forgiveness? No! Forgiveness is not about "them" or fairness or whether they deserve it. Forgiveness is about mercy. Jesus has a heart of mercy. We won't stand before God and answer for others; we will only answer for how we dealt with them. Did we show mercy?

I would like to share some practical exercises the Lord has taught me regarding forgiveness. Of course, the deeper the wound, the more difficult it is to forgive. An exercise that has helped me is to write out before the Lord the entire hurt I am dealing with, including everything that was said or happened. I then hold up the grievance before the Lord and thank Him for seeing all the details, pray for the person, and thank the Lord that I can trust Him to deal with this situation. Next, I either shred or burn the paper. It is so cleansing and cathartic to release our hurt. Writing it down and then giving it to the Lord is symbolic of our spiritual and emotional choice to leave it with Him.

▸What specific hurt came to mind as you read the paragraph above?

▸Take some time to write down the specific wound that came to mind. Then, prayerfully shred or burn the paper. How does this exercise make you feel?

A hurt that is deep may require more drastic measures. I had a deep childhood hurt, and I wanted to forgive, but my heart couldn't do it. My head kept saying "yes," but my heart was not moved to mercy. I encourage you, if you feel the Lord has called you to forgive a deep wound that you don't feel capable of forgiving, please consider fasting. In this particular case, I fasted for five days. At the end of the five days, I was completely broken. As I sat with the Lord, He revealed things to me about the person that I was unaware of, and He gave me mercy for that person. He broke the shackles of resentment and bitterness enchaining my heart.

This is what the Lord says, he who made the earth, the Lord who formed it and established it—the Lord is his name: "Call to me and I will answer you and tell you great and unsearchable things you do not know." (Jeremiah 33:2-3, NIV)

If you are stuck and feel you can't forgive some-one, please ask the Lord if He is calling you to fast and pray. I encourage you to check out Bill Bright's little booklet called "7 Basic Steps to Successful Fasting and Prayer".

▸Have you ever fasted? Will you consider asking the Lord if He would like you to fast in order to be free of any bitterness or resentment in your life?

Once we have chosen forgiveness, we have to choose selective memory. The enemy and our sin nature will push "play" on the tape in our thinking, replaying past hurts and sins. We must choose not to allow that tape to play over and over and say, "Thank You, Jesus, for taking care of that." We must ask the Holy Spirit to direct our thoughts toward what is good, admirable, and lovely.

Let the Spirit renew your thoughts and attitudes. (Ephesians 4:23, NLT)

And now, dear brothers and sisters, one final thing. Fix your thoughts on what is true, and honorable, and right, and pure, and lovely, and admirable. Think about things that are excellent and worthy of praise. (Philippians 4:8, NLT)

▸ Do your thoughts control you or do you control your thoughts?

▸ How can you contemplate more excellent, praise-worthy thoughts?

▸ How does what you listen to or read influence your thoughts?

Finally, as Christians, in an effort to seek peace, we confuse forgiveness with trust and restoration. Forgiveness does not mean we automatically trust the forgiven. Forgiveness is about me demonstrating mercy toward the other person. Trust, however, is earned; it is not freely given. If the offender seeks to restore the broken relationship, then trust can be restored. BUT, this is up to the offender. Restoration only happens when there is true repentance. We can be sorry and never change our behavior. Repentance requires making changes and being willing to rebuild the relationship. When someone wounds another, they burn a bridge that takes time and intentional effort to rebuild - a bridge of intimacy, honesty and trust. This only happens with true repentance and intentionality.

We sometimes think that if we forgive someone, we have to be friends with them again. This is not the case, some people are not safe and will continue to cause divisiveness and pain.

"And now, dear brothers and sisters, one final thing. Fix your thoughts on what is true, and honorable, and right, and pure, and lovely,and admirable. Think about things that are excellent and worthy of praise."

-Philippians 4:8, NLT

We must always choose forgiveness, but we cannot always choose restoration and trust. Our goal should be to restore the relationship, but if someone is struggling with addictions, a spirit of gossip, lying or divisiveness, they are not in a healthy place to seek restoration. In this case, you love them but keep healthy boundaries of distance.

Also, forgiveness does not mean we forget every sin. There are certain times when it is a sin to ignore actions committed by those who are divisive and fight against the kingdom of God. We must be on guard against allowing harmful behavior to continue. Paul wrote about this to Timothy.:

Alexander the metalworker did me a great deal of harm. The Lord will repay him for what he has done. You too should be on your guard against him, because he strongly opposed our message. (2 Timothy 4:14-15, NIV)

My husband and I were recently in Thailand, visiting a safe house for rescued, sex-trafficked children. I asked the founder how the children get to the place where they can forgive the evil traffickers who allowed unimaginable atrocities to happen to them. He said the mercy they displayed was a miracle, and only with Jesus was it even possible. He went on to tell me that many of the kids not only get to the place of total forgiveness but are so grateful for God's mercy in their lives, they want to extend mercy to the traffickers when they are arrested and are put on trial. They don't want to testify against their abusers; they want them to experience God's mercy!

Can you imagine that kind of mercy? I was astounded and shocked! These precious little ones truly understand the mercy of God. However, just as Paul warned Timothy about Alexander, the children are taught it would be wrong to forget the abuse and allow this sin to continue. They pray for the traffickers, but they strongly oppose the harm they cause and bravely testify against them.

These rescued children live out these words Paul wrote; "Be gentle and ready to forgive; never hold grudges. Remember, the Lord forgave you, so you must forgive others." (Colossians 3:13, TLB)

▸What one person do you need to forgive right now?

____

____

____

▸What gets in the way of trusting God and releasing that person into His capable hands?

____

____

____

Pray for that person. Maybe ask yourself this question, "If it weren't for this person, would I be happy?" That is the person you need to forgive. Ask God to let you see them through His eyes and make the deliberate choice to forgive them. Forgive the person who hurt you. Forgiveness is a choice, not an emotion or feeling. Forgiveness is a matter of the will, so we can all make that choice. If you make the choice to forgive, God will supply the mercy and forgiveness. Every time you think of that person, pray for God to bless them with His truth and His love, and your feelings will eventually change.

▸How will forgiving others impact your happiness and peace of mind?

____

____

____

We know we have chosen forgiveness if we can ask God to bless them.

Mother Theresa kept a copy of The Paradoxical Commandments on the wall of the orphanage she ran in Calcutta. The text brilliantly expresses the counter-intuitive nature of forgiveness; yet we are called on to act the opposite of how the world might expect in the face of continuous disappointment. Forgiveness is hard yet we are called to do it anyway. Where and in what ways can you act the opposite in your life?

THE PARADOXICAL COMMANDMENTS

by Dr. Kent M. Keith

PROBLEM	SOLUTION
People are illogical, unreasonable, and self-centered.	Love them anyway.
If you do good, people will accuse you of selfish ulterior motives.	Do good anyway.
If you are successful, you will win false friends and true enemies.	Succeed anyway.
The good you do today will be forgotten tomorrow.	Do good anyway.
Honesty and frankness make you vulnerable.	Be honest and frank anyway.
The biggest men and women with the biggest ideas can be shot down by the smallest men and women with the smallest minds.	Think big anyway.
People favor underdogs but follow only top dogs.	Fight for a few underdogs anyway.
What you spend years building may be destroyed overnight.	Build anyway.
People really need help but may attack you if you do help them.	Help people anyway.
Give the world the best you have and you'll get kicked in the teeth.	Give the world the best you have anyway.

video
TEACHING WEEK 4

What do we do with someone who doesn't recognize any wrong that has been done and isn't repenting and isn't asking for forgiveness?

"I, the LORD, made you, and I will not forget you.

I have swept away your sins like a cloud. I have scattered your offenses like the morning mist.

Oh, return to me, for I have paid the price to set you free." (Isaiah 44: 21-22)

Do you believe Abba Father has _______________ you of _______________ your sins?

Do you believe God's ____________________ is ____________________ than any sin you could commit?

Have you ____________________ and ____________________ forgiveness?

You and I cannot give someone something we have not chosen to ____________________.

Healthy, biblical forgiveness is about:

1) Perspective. Sometimes we need to lower our _______________________.

2) Punishment. Leave the ____________________ for bad behavior to __________________.

3) Purpose. God has specific ___________________ and ______________________ for you.

We _______________________ His plans when we don't _______________________.

"Never avenge yourselves. Leave that to God, for he has said that he will repay those who deserve it." (Romans 12:19, TLB)

WEEK

five

THE MERCIFUL TAKE ACTION

"Suppose someone has enough to live and sees a brother or sister in need, but does not help. Then God's love is not living in that person."

1 John 3:17, NCV

day one

What does it means to love in real life? It means to show another mercy. Whatever love we may think we have for others, if we are not dividing our bread with those in need, we are not loving the way God intended His children to love. One of my favorite authors, C.S. Lewis said, "It is easier to be enthusiastic about Humanity with a capital 'H' than it is to love individual men and women, especially those who are uninteresting, exasperating, depraved, or otherwise unattractive. Loving everybody in general may be an excuse for loving nobody in particular."

Goodness! When I read that quote it stabbed my heart.

‣Think of a difficult person in your life. How can you love them and show mercy to them?

The word "mercy" is used in the Bible to refer to God's actions toward us. Showing mercy is more than a momentary feeling of pity. Pity does nothing; mercy feels compassion and helps. Mercy described the actions and attitude of the early Church and was one reason it flourished; the early Church was moved to compassion by meeting individual needs and tragedies. Mercy does not say, "Oh, bless their hearts!" and move on by. Mercy means being willing to take the time to get inside their heads, hearts, and skin and to feel at some level what they are feeling. It means to act on their behalf; to see a need and to fulfill that need. The early believers were the first in their culture to sacrifice their own comfort in order to take in unwanted and abandoned children. They were the first to help care for the sick and the poor that society had discarded. These actions eventually led to the creation of Christian orphanages and hospitals all over the world.

‣How can you be an instrument to help ease someone's pain and suffering? Be specific.

You may have heard the saying, "If you are not feeling close to God, guess who moved?" I would add that if you want to see, feel and connect with Jesus, help someone in need.

‣When do you feel closest to Jesus?

When you are His instrument of healing and nourishment, whether physically or spiritually, you find and connect with Jesus. Mother Theresa made a profound statement, when she shared, "Each person I reach out to help is really Jesus in disguise."

What good is it, dear brothers and sisters, if you say you have faith but don't show it by your actions? Can that kind of faith save anyone? Suppose you see a brother or sister who has no food or clothing, and you say, "Good-bye and have a good day; stay warm and eat well"—but then you don't give that person any food or clothing. What good does that do?

So you see, faith by itself isn't enough. Unless it produces good deeds, it is dead and useless. (James 2:14-17, NLT)

‣How often do you encounter people in need? How do you respond?

"Whoever is kind to the poor lends to the LORD, and He will reward them for what they have done." (Proverbs 19:17, NIV)

Why don't we get involved? Why don't we show mercy by helping with our time and money? I think for the most part we want to help, but it is too easy to get distracted, turn a blind eye, and forget to take time for those in need. Unless we listen to the nudging of the Holy Spirit within us, we can become desensitized to the needs of others. The Lord gave me four reasons why we don't get involved. I certainly have been, and at times continue to be, guilty of all four. Remember, as we grow we become more like Him, and Jesus is incredibly merciful with us. None of us becomes a Christian and grow into His likeness overnight; it takes time and intentionality, and He is ever so patient with us. Please know the following points are not to make us feel guilty but rather to open our eyes to the abundant and purposeful life He has called us to enter into with Him and others.

One reason we don't show mercy is that we lack the desire to help. Have you noticed that people generally do what is comfortable for them? I have been serving in women's ministries for the past 20 years and have noticed that there is a direct correlation between those who are in God's Word and those who show mercy and care for others. Peter wrote that we ought to have the same thirst for the Word that babies have for their milk. Look again at the verse we studied in Week Two:

So get rid of all evil behavior. Be done with all deceit, hypocrisy, jealousy, and all unkind speech. Like newborn babies, you must crave pure spiritual milk so that you will grow into a full experience of salvation. Cry out for this nourishment, now that you have had a taste of the Lord's kindness. (1 Peter 2:1-3, NLT)

Notice how Peter connects the nourishment of God's Word in our souls with experiencing God's kindness (grace and mercy). Remember, the world does not offer mercy because the world does not have mercy to give. As followers of Christ, we are called to receive and give; receive from God and give to others. Loving God and loving others is our number one objective in this world. Why do we so often miss it?

God's word gives us the desire to love Him and others. Through His Word He shares His character with us and He is irresistible; to know Him is to love Him! It is through studying His Word that we discover who we are, why we are here, and where we are going.

▸How does your relationship with Jesus impact your desire to help others?

____

____

____

▸Spend some time in prayer, praying for the nourishment of "spiritual milk" that will help you grow.

____

____

‣On a scale of cold being a 1 and hot being a 10, where would you say your desire for Jesus is today?

I know you inside and out, and find little to my liking. You're not cold, you're not hot—far better to be either cold or hot! You're stale. You're stagnant. (Revelation 3:15-17, MSG)

God wrote to us in Revelation to return to Him. But I have this complaint against you. You don't love me or each other as you did at first! Look how far you have fallen! Turn back to me and do the works you did at first. If you don't repent, I will come and remove your lampstand from its place among the churches. (Revelation 2:4-5, NLT)

‣How do we return to God? How do we grow our desire to love Him and love others?

‣Which spiritual disciplines will grow your desire and love for Jesus?

TIPS FOR DRAWING CLOSER TO JESUS

Spend time singing and praising God.

Open His Word and read it.

Talk to Him throughout the day.

Call Him before calling others for help. Here is His number - 33:3, that is Jeremiah 33:3 (NKJV) "Call to Me, and I will answer you, and show you great and mighty things, which you do not know."

Fill your mind with great teachers of the Word. Check out Moody radio and their free app.

Choose to do life with those who love Jesus.

Start serving in your church.

Do you have a desire to help others? Are you a person of mercy? If you rarely consider helping those less fortunate, may I encourage you to start practicing the above disciplines?

God made you, and He knows how you function best. He desires the abundant, joyful, hopeful life for you, but you may never realize such a life if you are lukewarm toward Him and others.

Perhaps another reason we don't show mercy by offering our time or money is that we feel overwhelmed. There is so much need in this world. We may find ourselves becoming paralyzed and indifferent to it. Indifference puts up emotional walls, keeps us from feeling anything and drains all compassion. We say, "Why bother, we can't save the world?" When was the last time God asked you to save the world? He tells us He will not give us more than we can bear.

Before going to Thailand with Children's Hunger Fund, a Christian friend asked me why we were so involved with Children's Hunger Fund, since ". . . we certainly can't save all the starving and abused children in the world; the numbers are too overwhelming." One day at the safe house, as I watched the precious little boys and girls giggling and playing, I was overwhelmed with a feeling of gratitude that they were safe. Every face I looked at was worth helping. No, we can't save the world, but we can save one, two or maybe even thousands!

Hear my cry, O God; Attend to my prayer. From the end of the earth I will cry to You, when my heart is overwhelmed; lead me to the rock that is higher than I. (Psalm 61:1-2, NKJV)

You may feel overwhelmed, not knowing how you can use your God-given gifts to serve others. You can Google SHAPE by Pastor Rick Warren and listen to a great teaching that will help you determine how God wired you to serve. Then start doing something, such as get involved with your church's compassion ministries or your local homeless shelter, or your local senior citizen's home. Investigate trusted, Christ-centered organizations like Children's Hunger Fund, which seek to nourish the body and soul. It is great to feed a hungry body, but a soul is of eternal value!

▸ Who do you think the Lord wants you to help TODAY?

▸ What is one step you could take to show mercy in a practical and specific way to a specific person or group?

Children's Hunger Fund can feed a meal to a starving person for 25 cents, none of us can save the world, but each one of us can make a difference. You can make a difference!

Perhaps another reason we don't show mercy by offering our time or money is that we are too comfortable.

If you don't help others, it does not mean you are not a Christian; it just means you are not functioning as you should. It means you are not growing and transforming. Being comfortable can stagnate our walk with Jesus. Ezekiel declares: "Now this was the sin of your sister Sodom: She and her daughters were arrogant, overfed and unconcerned; they did not help the poor and needy. They were haughty and did detestable things before me . . . " (Ezekiel 16:49-50, NIV)

Striving to be comfortable leads a heart to be unconcerned with others. The daughters of Sodom were arrogant, overfed, and unconcerned; they did not help the poor and needy. Does this sound like the Western Christian to you? Yes, there are many amazing Christians who give generously of their time and treasures. However, if more of us were willing to forsake just a few comforts and indulgences, we could change the world! So many Christians can't be bothered with the rest of the world. Clearly, too many are unconcerned with 1.3 billion people who are starving.

Children's Hunger Fund advocate Mark Tatlock says many Christians live as "Functional Atheists". A Functional Atheist claims to be a Christian but lives for comforts and pleasures, not with a priority to glorify God and show mercy to the poor and unsaved.

The majority of the world's children do not live in safe places. The world's population is roughly 7.4 billion to date with almost 1.3 billion living on $1.25 a day and starving. We must pray for a merciful, compassionate heart. Do you want to be part of where the Spirit is moving?

▸Spend some time praying right now for God to lead you where His Spirit is moving—even if it means sacrificing your comfort.

Jesus had been given all power and authority, and we find Him washing the disciples' feet in John 13. He picked up a towel and washed feet.

Are you and I washing any feet?

▸Whom are you serving, other than yourself or your family?

Loving others can lead us to uncomfortable places.

A couple of years ago, my husband and I were in Burma, where I had the opportunity to teach Bible college students and pastors about studying God's Word and loving others. One of the ladies on our team shared how on a different mission trip, she washed all the people's feet who came to hear about the Lord. I can be a bit of a germaphobe, and as I looked around, I kept asking the Lord, "Do you literally want me to wash their feet?" I was pretty sure the answer was no, but the nudging of the Holy Spirit persisted.

When I could no longer shake His nudging, we gathered some supplies and washed their feet. My pastor washed the men's feet, and another lady and I washed the women's feet. These women walked many miles in the dirt with worn sandals. They were terribly embarrassed and didn't want us to wash their feet. I told them we were not leaving until they came forward and allowed us to pray over them and wash their feet. Finally, they pointed to the eldest and asked her to start. As they came forward, the Spirit moved within them, and they shared their personal stories of hardship and how they came to know Jesus as their Lord and Savior. Somehow, this act of mercy over them opened their hearts to want to connect with us on a deeper level.

I kept thinking these feet were like the feet Jesus washed–so worn, dirty, and tattered–and they belonged to a person whose story mattered. I have never met such humble, sweet souls hungry for Christ. Did that experience push me out of my comfort zone? Absolutely! However, the gift of connecting with Jesus through these beautiful Burmese women is a gift of love I will cherish forever. I have never felt so close to Him.

Jesus said, a new commandment I give you: love one another AS I HAVE LOVED YOU. We love and show mercy because He first loved us. Mercy is His Name.

It is so easy to run our errands; meet our friends for lunch, do our Bible studies, fold our fresh, clean laundry, shop in beautiful, clean markets with shelves full of food, care for our families, and not give a second thought to so many in need.

▸Who, other than your family, have you helped with your money or your time lately?

I believe the Lord longs to fill our hearts with mercy for others; we just need to ask for His help. No one can guilt you into a real desire to show mercy. A lasting desire to help comes from spending time with the Lord in His Word, recognizing His mercy in our lives, and then taking action! The more you reach out to help others, the more your desire to help grows.

He knows extending mercy to others will bring us incredible fulfillment. How many empty, unhappy Christians do you know? Life is too short to have a saved soul and a wasted life.

The Lord calls us out of our comfort zone to help others because this is when we grow. Growth is often painful and costs us something, but connecting with Jesus and loving on others is so worth it!

Let not mercy and truth forsake you; Bind them around your neck, Write them on the tablet of your heart. (Proverbs 3:3, NKJV)

Albert Barnes says, "Mercy is shutting out all forms of selfishness and hate. Truth is shutting out all forms of hypocrisy and falsehoods." No wonder our Lord desires us to write mercy and truth on the tablets of our hearts.

What we allow to be engraved on our hearts reflects the eye of our soul. It is who we have chosen to be and how we have chosen to live.

▸What do you think it means to write mercy and truth on the tablet of your heart? What would that look like?

The Bible says: When you're kind to others, you help yourself; when you're cruel to others, you hurt yourself. (Proverbs 11:17, MSG). How does being cruel to others hurt you?

Because we are made in God's image, our inner self approves of our kind and merciful acts toward others. Selfishness breeds jealousy, fear, suspicion, and pride, which lead to a hard, bitter heart. Studies have shown that the most joyful and peaceful people are those who are considerate and merciful with others.

A final reason we don't always choose to show mercy is we are too busy.

The Story of the Good Samaritan: Jesus taught that in order to have eternal life you must love the Lord with all your heart and soul, with all your strength and with your entire mind, and love your neighbor as yourself. And the question was posed, "Who is my neighbor?"

> Jesus, taking him up, replied, A certain man was going from Jerusalem down to Jericho, and he fell among robbers, who stripped him of his clothes and belongings and beat him and went their way, [unconcernedly] leaving him half dead, as it happened. Now by coincidence a certain priest was going down along that road, and when he saw him, he passed by on the other side. A Levite [someone who served in the Temple or as we would say someone in ministry] likewise came down to the place and saw him, and passed by on the other side [of the road]. But a certain Samaritan, as he traveled along, came down to where he was; and when he saw him, he was moved with pity and sympathy [for him]. . . .
>
> Which of these three do you think proved himself a neighbor to him who fell among the robbers? He answered, The one who showed pity and mercy to him. And Jesus said to him, "Go and do likewise." (Luke 10: 30-33, 36-37, AMP)

The Good Samaritan demonstrated mercy. He didn't wait for a committee to be formed to help the needy by the road, and he didn't wait for the injured man to ask for help. He saw a need in front of him, and he took action. He also gave freely of his time and money to help.

As Christians and as humans, this doesn't mean we can or should be everything to everybody. We can't fulfill every need that falls in our path. The Samaritan didn't establish a foundation or set up an aid station for imperiled travelers. But he did respond to what he could; the need was plainly and undeniably before him. He fulfilled his responsibility, both socially and spiritually. As the 19th century theologian Alexander Maclaren pointed out, "The world would be a changed place if every Christian attended to the sorrows that are plain before him."

So often, we can't afford any interruptions in our day because we are busy, busy, busy. The Priest and the Levite were busy with their teaching, counseling, and music ministries; they didn't have time to help. They had to go pray, teach or sing in the Temple. Notice Jesus did not condemn the robbers, although stealing is one of the biggies mentioned in the Ten Commandments. He went a level deeper to demonstrate the heart of God and condemned those in the House of God who could not be bothered by someone else's needs.

Alexander Maclaren, Expositions of Holy Scripture, The Gospel of St. Luke, 1892, public domain.

▸ Describe a time your schedule was interrupted by someone who needed a listening ear or a shoulder to cry on. How did you respond? What happened?

____

____

____

____

It could be as simple as looking into someone's eyes and making them feel as though what they are saying really matters. It could be as simple as seeing someone cry in the aisle of Target and asking her if she is okay, hearing her out, and asking if you could pray for her.

Making ourselves available will sometimes cause us a bit of anxiety and sacrifice. During a very busy time in my life, when my two children were attending different schools, a friend asked me to help a mom we knew from our kids' elementary days. Linda's husband had recently died, and she was fighting stage four cancer. She was alone with no family to help her. At the time my plate was overflowing with many commitments and two kids with busy schedules. How could I squeeze in taking dinner to Linda and also spend time with her once or twice a week? I was busy! The Holy Spirit kept nudging me to be compassionate and supportive despite my busy schedule.

There were many nights when I was anxiously racing to her house, but I always came away with a renewed calm, knowing I was doing exactly what the Lord had called me to do. She was a precious, grateful soul, and she often encouraged me with her peace and hope, even though she was suffering.

Blessed are the merciful. I was really the one blessed. God blessed me. "Whoever is kind to the poor lends to the LORD, and He will reward them for what they have done." (Proverbs 19:17, NIV)

As my friends and I assisted Linda, the Lord gave us an amazing gift. As the end was drawing near, I was reading her some Scriptures about heaven. I chose passages from Revelation, describing how glorious heaven is. As I was reading (she was unresponsive, not moving or talking by now), she sat straight up in bed, reached up and held her arms open wearing the biggest smile you have ever seen. My friends and I froze; how could she sit up? What was she looking at as she stared up at the ceiling? What was the divinely, peaceful, joyful look on her face?

The hospice nurse walked us to our car and shared with us that it is not uncommon for the Lord to give a glimpse of Glory to His dying one. We witnessed something supernatural that day! She saw something so glorious that she reached out for it in anticipation and we were blessed to witness it!

"Do not withhold good from those who deserve it when it's in your power to help them." (Proverbs 3:27, NLT)

▸ Who needs help today that you have the power to provide?

____

____

____

Mercy bears fruit; the fruit of joy, hope and peace.

video TEACHING WEEK 5

Three points on mercy from the Good Samaritan Parable found in Luke 10:25-37 (ESV)

1. Mercy has ________________________ to see a wide range of ________________________ is in need.

   A Samaritan, as he journeyed, came to where he was; and he saw him (Luke 10:33, ESV). How big is your mercy circle of vision?

2. Mercy has a ________________________ that is filled with compassion and loving-kindness toward a person in need.

   When he saw him, he had compassion on him. (Luke 10:33 ESV). Don't look out only for your own interests, but take an interest in others, too (Philippians 2:4, NLT).

3. Mercy responds by ________________________ to help.

"He went to him and bound up his wounds, pouring oil and wine; then he set him on his own beast and brought him to an inn, and took care of him." (Luke 10:34 ESV) "Sodom's sins were pride, gluttony, and laziness, while the poor and needy suffered outside her door." (Ezekiel 16:49, NLT).

"We are most like Christ when we choose to offer the gift of our presence and choose to absorb within ourselves the suffering of the least, the last, and the lost. Are you looking for Jesus? That is where you will find Him."
– Kay Warren

WEEK

six

THE MERCIFUL ARE GENEROUS GIVERS

"We were made to both give and to forgive. Paul's last words to the church of Ephesus were, "And I have been a constant example of how you can help those in need by working hard. You should remember the words of the Lord Jesus: 'It is more blessed to give than to receive.'"

Acts 20:35, NLT

Our lives here on earth are like a pebble falling in a lake: a plop and then we are gone. "You are a mist that appears for a little while and then vanishes." (James 4:14b, NIV) However, because we are children of a living God, even small acts of giving can cause ripple effects that last throughout eternity.

Christianity spread like wild fire through the ancient world because Christians were different; they invited others into their homes and gave much. There was a common saying during the early years of Christianity that although they did not share a common bed, they shared a common table. They looked very different than the rest of the world; they had different morals and freely gave what they could to help others. The United States of America, a nation founded and rooted in Christian principles, is the most generous nation in the world. Our family lived in Spain for a year and had the opportunity to meet many Europeans. I always asked them, "What is the first thing that comes to mind, when you think of Americans?" Everywhere we went the answer was the same; they said we are the friendliest, loudest, and most generous people. Many shared how they found it fascinating that when disaster befalls another nation, Americans are always the first to show up to help. We are the first to send relief. God bless America!

▸What does being generous mean to you?

____

____

____

The dictionary's definition of "generous" is: showing a readiness to give more of something, as money or time, than is necessary or expected.

I love these words to describe being generous: merciful, bighearted, bountiful, freehearted, openhanded, hospitable, openhearted, compassionate, good-hearted, abundant, and kind.

▸Would those who know you say you are a generous person? Explain.

____

____

____

If the answer to the above question is "No," don't fret! Ask Abba Father in Jesus' name to open your eyes to His provisions in your life. As we realize more and more how incredibly blessed we are in Christ, our heart of generosity grows. Our entire time here is meant to grow us more and more into His image. Babies don't walk over night; they grow into first walking and then running.

The more time we spend with our generous, Merciful and loving Savior, the clearer our path will be and we will run the race marked out for us. Don't be too hard on yourself during this transformative process.

Christ first gave to us; The Book of Acts says it like this: "We are saved because the Master Jesus amazingly and out of sheer generosity moved to save us" (Acts 15:11, MSG). Thank you, Jesus! Amen!!!

God is ever so generous with us. Everything we have is because of His generosity, including the air we breathe. Paul wrote to the believers in Corinth: "What do you have that God hasn't given you?" (1 Corinthians 4:7, NLT) And our God gives in abundance, unlike our great Adversary. "The thief comes only to steal and kill and destroy. I came that they may have life and have it to the full." (John 10:10, NIV)

However in his letter to the Galatians, Paul does make his point very clear: "Don't be misled: No one makes a fool of God. What a person plants, he will harvest. The person who plants selfishness, ignoring the needs of others—ignoring God!—harvests a crop of weeds. All he'll have to show for his life is weeds! But the one who plants in response to God, letting God's Spirit do the growth work in him, harvests a crop of real life, eternal life." (Galatians 6:7-8, MSG)

What we plant, we will harvest; what we sow, we will reap. We know if we plant tomato seeds, we will not harvest corn. Abba Father created the universe, and He created you. The real you, created in His image, is a giver. Abba has been incredibly giving toward us, and when we are giving toward others, He is quite pleased. We will harvest an inner joy and a peace we can't obtain if we are primarily focused on meeting only our needs.

‣ How are you planting seeds in your life in response to God?

‣ What harvest have you seen in your own life when you give?

Jesus tells us, "Don't store up treasures here on earth, where moths eat them and rust destroys them, and where thieves break in and steal. Store your treasures in heaven, where moths and rust cannot destroy, and thieves do not break in and steal." (Matthew 6:19-20, NLT) When we invest in others by giving either our time or money to help them, we are not only making a difference on this earth, we are also investing in our eternity. Showing mercy is an investment that has a very high rate of return!

day two

I love worshipping our God. He is so merciful and generous with us.

Theologian Adam Clarke said, "Our afflictions we scarcely ever forget; our mercies we scarcely ever remember! Our hearts are alive to complaint, but dead to gratitude. We have had ten thousand mercies for one judgment, and yet our complaints to our thanksgivings have been ten thousand to one! How is it that God endures this and bears with us?"

He endures and bears with us because He overflows with mercy and generosity toward us, and He wants us to know we can trust Him with our lives. God wrote these words to YOU: "The Lord is pleased with those who respect him, with those who trust his love." (Psalm 147:11, NCV) He wants the very best for us. This is His promise to us: "Take delight in the Lord, and he will give you the desires of your heart" (Psalm 37:4, NIV).

The most important decision we make, after receiving Jesus as our Savior, is to choose to know Him, trust Him and delight in His ways. When we do this, then He takes great pleasure in us because we are doing what is right. Then we can be at peace with ourselves because as Zephaniah 3:17 says, "The Lord your God . . . will take great delight in you, He will quiet you with His love, He will rejoice over you with singing." (NIV)

‣How does someone act when they have a reverent fear and respect for the Lord?

‣How do you express your delight in the Lord?

‣When you read that the Lord "takes great delight in you," what thoughts or feelings come to you? In what ways have you experienced God's delight?

Commentary on the Bible, 1832, public domain

One of my favorite scriptures is found in Ephesians 2:4 (NLT) "But God is so rich in mercy, and he loved us so much." This sums up why Abba Father bears with us. He loves us so much!

▸What barriers get in the way of receiving Abba Father's love? What holds you back from fully embracing His love for you?

Taking great delight in the Lord and accepting His love and mercy in our lives moves us to give to others. We want to share all that we have been blessed with by God. Why? Because generous giving is an indicator that you understand that everything you have is because of God's mercy and generosity toward you. John Wesley said, "Not, how much of my money will I give to God, but how much of God's money will I keep for myself."

God has blessed you, and He desires you to be a blessing. There is no greater joy than to be a blessing to others; this is how our Creator wired us. He knows the deep desires of our heart before we uncover them. When He was giving Moses the principles for Godly living to share with the people before entering the Promised Land, the Lord said, "No one should appear before the Lord empty-handed: Each of you must bring a gift in proportion to the way the Lord your God has blessed you" (Deuteronomy 16: 16b-17, NIV).

And later Paul wrote to the believers, "And God will generously provide all you need. Then you will always have everything you need and plenty left over to share with others." (2 Corinthians 9:8, NLT). Paul also wrote to us, "You are daughters of Day. So let's not sleepwalk through life like those others. Let's keep our eyes open and be smart" (1Thessalonians 5: 4-8, MSG).

▸What does it mean to "sleepwalk through life," particularly when it comes to generosity?

John Wesley. AZquotes.com, Wind and Fly LTD, 2017

Don't you just love how our God is not a God of confusion? If He wants us to understand an important principle of Godly living, He repeats it throughout His Word and explains it clearly. There are three important principles regarding generous giving that He shares with us:

1. GIVE NOW

Time has a moral significance to us Christians. In Ephesians 5:16-17, Paul wrote, "Make the most of every opportunity in these evil days. Don't act thoughtlessly, but understand what the Lord wants you to do." (NLT) Paul's message is: Don't waste your God-given time on being busy, but make the most of every chance you get.

Do you feel a sense of urgency and responsibility in doing God's work? It is not hearing from God that changes our lives. It is applying and doing what we hear from God that changes our lives: "But be doers of the word, and not hearers only, deceiving yourselves" (James 1:22, NKJV).

‣ What happens to us when we hear and even agree with God's word but don't practice it?

Truth is for now, not for later or when you are in a better place. God is not impressed with good intentions. Perhaps you have heard the saying, "The road to hell is paved with good intentions." Obedience today is the greatest preparation for tomorrow. Give NOW. Don't wait. It is interesting how many Christians have said to me, "When I have more money, I will start giving." The truth is, giving is not a matter of how much money you have; it is a matter of the heart. People who give when they have little will give more when they have more, and people who don't give when they have little will not give, when they have plenty.

Command those who are rich in this present world not to be arrogant nor to put their hope in wealth, which is so uncertain, but to put their hope in God, who richly provides us with everything for our enjoyment.Command them to do good, to be rich in good deeds, and to be generous and willing to share. In this way they will lay up treasure for themselves as a firm foundation for the coming age, so that they may take hold of the life that is truly life. (1 Timothy 6:17-19, NIV)

‣ Practically, how do you show your invisible God to others by giving generously?

Generosity resembles Godly character. Mercy responds. Mercy follows up. Mercy has a generous spirit and makes you feel as though you matter. When you give to someone in need, you create a connection with that person. Hopefully, that connection will eventually connect them to Christ.

▸Can you think of a time someone gave their time or money to you? How did that impact your connection with that person?

___

___

___

The Lord calls us to make the most of every opportunity to be generous now. He also desires us to give in the following way:

2. GIVE JOYFULLY

I used to always tell my kids, "It's not always what you say but how you say it." How we do things matters, and we don't ever want to compromise our witness by doing the right thing the wrong way. How does the Lord desire us to give? Paul tells us in 2 Corinthians 9:7, "Each of you should give what you have decided in your heart to give, not reluctantly or under compulsion, for God loves a cheerful giver."(NIV)

Author Christian Smith, in his book The Paradox of Generosity: Giving We Receive, Grasping We Lose, cites research by Notre Dame's William R. Kenan Jr., Professor of Sociology, and sociology doctoral candidate Hilary Davidson, that shows giving gives us joy. According to their research, people who ". . . give money generously, volunteer their time, and are overall a generous neighbor and friend . . . have significant and noticeable more personal happiness, better physical health [and] a stronger sense of purpose."

The report further states: "by failing to care for others, we do not properly take care of ourselves...It is no coincidence that the word 'miser' is derived from the word 'miserable.'" The Lord is inviting us into His generous life, and when we accept the invitation, the party favor He gives is joy.

▸What next step is the Lord inviting you to take in order to be a part of His generous living?

___

___

___

His master replied, "Well done, good and faithful servant! You have been faithful with a few things; I will put you in charge of many things. Come and share your master's happiness!" (Matthew 25:21, NIV)

You can read the whole parable in Matthew 25, but the lesson is about three men who were given three different amounts of money to manage for their Master. They were all given exactly what they could handle, according to their abilities, and they were held accountable for how they used and shared their resources. Two men did the best they could with their resources. They were told, "Well done, good and faithful servant!" The third man did nothing (he buried his money), and the Master called him wicked and lazy. We can't ignore or squander what the Lord has given us.

▸Why is it so easy to behave like the third servant and give nothing to others?

___

___

___

Smith, Christian and Davidson, Hilary. The Paradox of Generosity: Giving We Receive, Grasping We Lose. New York: Oxford University Press, 2014.

3. GIVE GENEROUSLY

How generous are we Americans? The average individual income in the world is $2.50 a day. Billions of people cannot imagine turning a lever and having a hot shower or being able to brush their teeth with toothpaste, or walk into a beautiful market full of food. Again referring to The Paradox of Generosity: Giving We Receive, Grasping We Lose, Kenan and David's research found that "only 2.7 percent of Americans gave a 10th or more of their income to charity, at least 86.2 percent give away less than 2 percent of their income and nearly half give nothing."

This research is especially sad when we consider how generous America is compared to the rest of the world. It seems obvious that, by nature, most of us are not generous. God says He loves it when we choose to grow in generous giving, and He even promises blessings along the way.

"Good will come to those who are generous and lend freely." (Psalm 112:5, NIV). Only when we open our hands wide can the Lord place His blessings in them. This is not to be confused with the false Prosperity Gospel, which teaches financial blessing and physical well-being are always the will of God for us. I always wonder what Bible they are reading because our Savior was not wealthy on earth, and he certainly did not have physical well-being, nor did His disciples. God is much more concerned with my growth than my comfort. The benefits and blessings He promises us, when we are generous, are usually referring to the good of our soul–the real us, the eternal us. There are no material possessions, indulgences, or comforts that compare with peace, joy, purpose, hope, and a vision for the future.

When we are willing to give, we demonstrate to others and ourselves that our faith does not depend on material possessions. Instead, we show that our faith is in Jehovah Jireh.

‣ How would you rate the spiritual maturity of those who give generously? Explain.

____

____

____

‣ In what areas can you decrease your spending and increase your giving?

____

____

____

Giving isn't an issue of income; it is an issue of the heart.

Should people cheat God? Yet you have cheated me! But you ask, 'What do you mean? When did we ever cheat you?' "You have cheated me of the tithes and offerings due to me. You are under a curse, for your whole nation has been cheating me. Bring all the tithes into the storehouse so there will be enough food in my Temple. If you do," says the Lord of Heaven's Armies, "I will open the windows of heaven for you. I will pour out a blessing so great you won't have enough room to take it in! Try it! Put me to the test!"(Malachi 3:8-10, NLT)

One of the most misquoted verses in the Bible is "money is the root of all evil." In actuality, the verse says "the love of money is the root of all evil" (1 Timothy 6:10, NLT). Money itself is neutral; it is neither good nor bad. It is what we choose to do with our money that is good or bad. As we discussed in day three, a person who is generous with a little is even more generous with a lot, and a person who is selfish with little is also selfish with a lot. Money just makes us more of who we already are.

‣Why do you think Paul wrote, "For the love of money is the root of all kinds of evil?" (You may want to read the context of 1 Timothy 6:10)

Jesus taught about using wealth to help the needy. The rich man who claimed to have followed all the commandments and wanted to know how to get eternal life (Matthew 19), the parable of the rich fool (Luke 12:13-21), and the rich man and Lazarus parable (Luke 16:19-31) all share something in common: in these parables the rich men are NOT criticized for their wealth but for their neglect of the poor. Their sin was forgetting that God was the true source of their wealth.

You and I can make a difference. Let's ask the Lord to show us where He wants us to give. "The Lord replies, 'I have seen violence done to the helpless, and I have heard the groans of the poor. Now I will rise up to rescue them, as they have longed for me to do.'" (Psalm 12:5, NLT) We want to be where His Spirit is moving, and He is moving among the needy, the forgotten, the marginalized, and the poor (both the poor in immediate needs as well as the poor in spirit). We all want to stand before Him and hear Him say,

"Well done, good and faithful servant." Right?

Then the King will answer, 'I tell you the truth, anything you did for even the least of my people here, you also did for me.' (Matthew 25:40, NCV)

‣How does God want us to respond to His mercy and generosity toward us?

Imitate God, therefore, in everything you do, because you are His dear children. (Ephesians 5:1, NLT)

Remember, if Children's Hunger Fund can feed a starving person for 25 cents, we can all make a difference!

I would like to leave you with a passage that has gotten me through many struggles. It reminds me of Abba's incredible mercy. Perhaps you know it. If not, may I encourage you to write these ancient, timeless Divine Words on the tablet of your heart?

The Lord is my shepherd; I shall not want. He makes me to lie down in green pastures; He leads me beside the still waters. He restores my soul; He leads me in the paths of righteousness For His name's sake. Yea, though I walk through the valley of the shadow of death, I will fear no evil; For You are with me; Your rod and Your staff, they comfort me. You prepare a table before me in the presence of my enemies; You anoint my head with oil; My cup runs over. Surely goodness and mercy shall follow me all the days of my life; And I will dwell in the house of the Lord forever. (Psalm 23, NKJV)

Amen!

Check out childrenshungerfund.org/donate/

"For the love of money is the root of all kinds of evil. Some people, eager for money, have wandered from the faith and pierced themselves with many griefs."

-1 Timothy 6:10

video TEACHING WEEK 6

Why is surrendering our financial lives to God so hard for us?

"And God will generously provide all you need. Then you will always have everything you need and plenty left over to share with others." (2 Corinthians 9:8)

Generosity means being a person of ________________________.

Generosity is not just an ________________________, it is a ________________________.

We are called to be generous in ________________________ area of life:

1) The merciful are generous with their ______________. Everything we have and manage is a ____________ from ______________.

"Don't store treasures for yourselves here on earth where they will be destroyed. But store your treasures in heaven where they cannot be destroyed." (Matthew 6:19-20)

2) The merciful are generous with their ______________.

My dear children, let's not talk about love; let's practice real love. This is the only way we'll know we're living truly, living in God's reality. (Matthew 6:19-20)

3) The merciful are generous with their ________________.

"Stir up the gift of God which is in you; keep it burning, fan into a flame. And the special gift of ministry you received when I laid hands on you and prayed—keep that ablaze! God doesn't want us to be shy with his gifts, but bold and loving and sensible." (2 Timothy 1: 6-7)

Do you know what your spiritual gifts are? Where are you being generous with those gifts?

"There are three conversations necessary for the Christian: the conversation of the heart, the mind, and the purse." -Martin Luther